THIS ITEM HAS BEEN
DISCARDED BY THE
UNIVERSITY OF PUGET SOUND
COLLINS MEMORIAL LIBRARY

Johnsonian
*and Other Essays
and Reviews*

Johnsonian
and Other Essays
and Reviews

BY
R. W. CHAPMAN

OXFORD
AT THE CLARENDON PRESS
1953

Republished 1971
Scholarly Press, Inc., 22929 Industrial Drive East
St. Clair Shores, Michigan 48080

Library of Congress Catalog Card Number: 78-158502
ISBN 0-403-01297-X

Preface

IN collecting these *Ephemera* I have made no attempt to bring them up to date. I have corrected some mistakes, deleted some irrelevances, mitigated some asperities, and explained some obscure allusions.

I am a mere amateur of typography, but in reviving *The Art of Printing* I bow to the injunction, long since expressed, of Mr. Bruce Rogers.

R. W. C.

Nov. 1952

Contents

Samuel Johnson	1
Johnson's Reputation	7
The Making of the 'Life of Johnson'	20
Johnson and Poetry	37
Landscape Gardening	54
The Art of Printing	71
Textual Criticism	83
Thomas Love Peacock	96
Oliver Goldsmith, 1728(?)–1774	104
Chesterfield's Letters	115
Lexicography	126
S.P.E.: Retrospect	147

OTHER REVIEWS

Poetic Diction	159
Sir Walter Raleigh's Letters	162
Percy and Goldsmith	170
Aspects of Johnson	174

Contents

OTHER REVIEWS (*continued*)

Boswell without Johnson	182
Boswell without Malone	186
Johnson and Queeney	192
Jane Austen	197
To What Strange Shores?	202
The Yale Walpole	214
"Oτι's Business	232
The New Smith	239

v

Samuel Johnson[1]

WE are met to commemorate the anniversary of the death of Samuel Johnson, who died near this place on the 13th of December 1784. That he would have disapproved the purpose of our assembly is, I think, probable, but need not disturb us. The scruples which might have vexed him 142 years ago are scruples which he would not feel if he were alive today. In saying this I have already touched the secret of that domination which awed his contemporaries, and which has compelled our presence here. Johnson is still in Fleet Street. He has not become obsolete.

It is right to ask ourselves why we celebrate this occasion in this way. Perhaps no two Johnsonians will give quite the same answer. There are indeed certain obvious proprieties which we all feel. Johnson was a great Englishman, a great Londoner, and a great Churchman. Yet these, I think, are rather the accidents than the substance. Johnson is not a great imaginative writer. He does not, like Shakespeare, lead us into those dark places of the soul which we could not explore without a poet's aid. He does not, like Plato or like Shelley, transport us into brighter regions, or show us the spirit of man loosed from earthly shackles. Nor does he, like Wordsworth, take us apart into great spaces, or teach us to commune with the God of Nature in temples not made with hands. He is no magician; he is only Samuel Johnson, a moral writer.

[1] An address delivered at St. Clement Danes on 13 December 1926.

Samuel Johnson

Even his morality has little that strikes by its novelty. His maxims are, for the most part, general and familiar, and seem to tell us little that every man may not discover for himself. But all precepts of morality, if they rest on the common sense of mankind, are of this nature. They are as new as they are old, and remain empty of meaning until they are recharged by experience. Johnson's morality does not quickly give up the secret of its greatness. You can make a valuable book of aphorisms out of Boswell or the *Rambler*; but when it is made it is not quite Johnson. It is only by familiarity with the mass of his recorded wisdom, and by testing its application to life, that we come to perceive the breadth of knowledge and depth of insight that give his judgements their weight and force.

Let us endeavour [he writes to a friend] to see things as they are, and then enquire whether we ought to complain. Whether to see life as it is will give us much consolation, I know not; but the consolation which is drawn from truth, if any there be, is solid and durable; that which may be derived from error must be, like its original, fallacious and fugitive.

The author of this advice was a man whom life had not used kindly. He was left, in middle age, a childless widower, with no relations, and few friends of his own generation. He had always been poor. He had never known health, or the ineffaceable delights of a happy childhood. His marriage we may believe yielded such happiness as its circumstances permitted. Otherwise his pleasures arose from the satisfaction of intellectual curiosity, and from that knowledge of his powers which the contests of Fleet Street afforded. But he knew that 'it is the business of a wise man to be happy';

and he knew very well what are the true sources of human felicity.

His depreciation of love, as an ingredient in dramatic literature, is notorious: 'Love is only one of many passions; and as it has no great influence on the sum of life, it has little operation in the drama of a poet who caught his ideas from the living world.' But you remember what happened to the lady who, seeking to draw him, derided the novels of the day because they treated of love: 'We must not ridicule a passion which he who never felt never was happy, and he who laughs at never deserves to feel—a passion which has caused the change of empires and the loss of worlds—a passion which has inspired heroism and subdued avarice.'

'The basis of all excellence is truth.' The qualities in which Johnson's superiority to common men is most conspicuous are his truthfulness, and the courage which empowers him to apprehend and face truth, however forbidding. He never shirked what he called 'the pain of being a man'. Of the pains of humanity, in this sense, not the least acute is the recognition of our own selfish loneliness. Johnson saw it without flinching. No one felt more acutely than he the loss of a friend; but he listened with impatience to any exaggerated expression of grief; for, said he, 'we must either outlive our friends, you know, or our friends must outlive us; and I see no man that would hesitate about the choice'. But his rejection of those pretences and evasions by which it is sought to make life seem better than it is never betrayed him to bitterness. As a young man, he confesses, 'I was much inclined to treat mankind with asperity and contempt; but I found it answered no good end. I thought it wiser and better to take the world as it goes.' He early learned the wisdom of tolerance, of which his life of Richard Savage is the immortal expression.

But Johnson has other qualities, without which these moral and intellectual virtues, though they must command our admiration, would hardly enlist our affections. The gifts which place him in the front rank of human wisdom are his abounding love for his fellows, and his invincible faith in the nobility of our nature. It is this faith which gives light and splendour to those other virtues of fortitude, resignation and sincerity; which makes him, not a sturdy Stoic, but a great Christian.

For this faith it is not easy to furnish texts. Boswell found its clearest expression in that passage of the *Rambler* on 'Pain', which, he tells us, he could never read 'without feeling his frame thrill'.

> I think there is some reason for questioning whether the body and mind are not so proportioned that the one can bear all that can be inflicted on the other; whether virtue cannot stand its ground as long as life, and whether a soul well principled will not be separated sooner than subdued.

We may find the same faith in Johnson's considered opinion, that 'Want of tenderness is want of parts, and is no less a proof of stupidity than of depravity'; or in his description of his own times, as 'an age which, amidst all its vices and all its follies, has not become infamous for want of charity'. But we need not look for any formal *Credo*; Johnson's belief in the dignity of human nature informed his life. The passionate intensity of his conviction rang out, again and again, in unforgettable sentences which are the glory of English prose.

I have said that Johnson is not, in the highest sense, a poet. His religion is not a religion of joy. He has no message for children or for lovers. But the high themes of poetry, though they are the essence of life, are not its bulk. The greater part of the lives of most of us is given to toil, perplexity, and compromise. We are chained to earth and to our fellow sufferers. Of that part of life the old philosopher can help to ease the burden; not indeed by distraction—for he never takes us, as we say, 'out of ourselves'; but by that 'bark and steel for the mind' which his writings and his talk afford. He will not let us soften the facts in our favour—he will always insist that we 'clear our *minds* of cant'. We feel that he knows the worst; but we are confident that his understanding and his charity will not fail.

To the life of Fleet Street his wisdom and experience are peculiarly apt. For he knew every phase of the profession of letters and journalism, and every day supplies us with situations that evoke his piercing, illuminating comment. In our highly conservative society it seems likely that this celebration of the Johnson Anniversary, once instituted, will be long continued. His disciples may, I think, with great propriety honour his memory in the church in which he worshipped. We know his opinion of the value of books: they should teach us 'how best to enjoy life, or how best to bear it'. If, under the open sky, by the sea, or among mountains, we turn to literature for comfort or for inspiration, a right instinct sends us to the poets. Here, in Fleet

Samuel Johnson

Street, among the human traditions and the grime of a great city, in the centre of 'a world that is bursting with sin and sorrow', we are content to thank God for Samuel Johnson.

Johnson's Reputation[1]

THE history of Johnson's reputation is accurately reflected in his bibliography. In his lifetime, when once the Dictionary had secured his fame, his books were in steady though never in very great demand. Of the *Rambler* some eleven editions were printed between 1752 and 1784. There were seven lifetime editions of *Rasselas*. *The Lives of the Most Eminent English Poets*, completed in 1781, was reprinted in the same year, and again in 1783. When Johnson died, the booksellers combined to produce a collected edition, and this was published in eleven volumes in 1787. The editor was Sir John Hawkins, who prefixed to the collection a lengthy *Life* of his friend, which is now seldom read though it has been used as a quarry by later builders.

Hawkins's edition was incomplete; and two booksellers, not members of the original group, made haste to supplement it by printing the *Parliamentary Debates*, the translation of Lobo, and a number of miscellaneous pieces: in all four volumes, which were offered to 'those Gentlemen who intend to complete Dr. Johnson's Works'. About the same time George Strahan published *Prayers and Meditations composed by Samuel Johnson*; the Rev. Samuel Hayes, Usher of Westminster School, published *Sermons on Different Subjects, left for publication by John Taylor, LL.D. . . . to which is added a Sermon written by Samuel Johnson, LL.D., for the Funeral of his Wife*—a juxtaposition intended to point the ambiguity of *left for publication*. Mrs. Piozzi published *Letters to and from*

[1] *The Times Literary Supplement*, 1 Sept. 1921.

Johnson's Reputation

the late Samuel Johnson, LL.D., and other letters appeared in *The Gentleman's Magazine*. The Poems also were separately collected.

The demand of which these publications are proof was not quickly satisfied. The Works of Samuel Johnson, LL.D., continued to be printed at frequent intervals for nearly forty years. Hawkins's *Life*, indeed, and his arrangement of the *Works* did not commend themselves; an *Essay* by Arthur Murphy replaced the *Life*, and the edition of 1792 in twelve volumes to which it was prefixed became the standard. It was reissued, with occasional corrections and amplifications, in 1796, 1801, 1810, 1816, 1823, 1824. Another edition was printed in ten volumes in 1818; and in 1825 appeared no fewer than four editions: Talboys' edition, still called the best, in nine volumes, Lynam's in six, another in two, and an edition printed at Philadelphia. Upon this *crescendo* the curtain falls. The *Works* have not been printed since, save in the comprehensive collection of Bohn, and more recently by an enterprising book company of Troy, N.Y. And indeed there is no necessity; for there are many more copies in the second-hand shops than there are patrons of literature willing to spare Johnson two feet of shelf-room.

The bibliography of Johnson's life and talk tells a different story. The publication of his oral wit and wisdom began in his lifetime, with the appearance in 1766 of *Johnsoniana; or, a Collection of Bon Mots, &c. By Dr. Johnson, and Others*. A great part of this very ordinary jest-book is not Johnson; the choice of title is, however, significant. The book was reprinted, with additions, in the following year. Johnson called it 'a mighty impudent thing'; and in anticipation of the theme of this article, shook his head over its popularity. Being told it had sold very well, 'Yet the *Journey to the Hebrides*', said he, 'has not had a great sale.'

Boswell is often credited with having wished to publish his Journal of the Hebridean Tour when Johnson published his own *Journey* in 1775; but the evidence for this seems to be slender. If he had such aspirations, Johnson deterred him. Beyond the 'impudent' *Johnsoniana*, there seems to have been no further revelation of the philosopher at his ease, until death removed the barriers of decency and let loose a stream of anecdote. The magazines of 1785 and 1786 are full of reminiscences. Sir John Hawkins was appointed official biographer—not a happy choice. But before his ponderous volume could appear rivals were already in the field. More than one *Life* was hastily put together, at the instance, no doubt, of enterprising booksellers. Boswell had only to prepare his *Journal* for the press—an earnest of the greater work, for which he now announced that he had 'been collecting materials for more than twenty years, during which he was honoured with the intimate friendship of Dr. Johnson'. Mrs. Piozzi had only to consult a retentive memory to produce the entertaining *Anecdotes*, which were for some years the most popular of the *Johnsoniana*.

Boswell's *Life* was not published until 1791. It immediately assumed the place which it still holds. It displaced all its rivals and forerunners—except Boswell's own *Hebrides*, which is indeed an integral part of it—and they are now read, if they are read, as supplement and commentary to Boswell. The author lived to produce a second edition and to make collections for a third; and when he died, Edmond

Johnson's Reputation

Malone—who had taken a hand from the first—assumed the office of editing 'one of the most instructive and entertaining works in the English language'. Malone produced four editions, and the work was gradually enriched by the insertion of fresh documents and of notes by various hands. This process was carried further by Croker, who in his edition of 1831 intercalated the *Tour* in its chronological place—a liberty which Macaulay condemned—and added a wealth of illustrative matter. Croker also collected from contemporary memoirs and other sources the extensive supplement of *Johnsoniana*, long afterwards edited and expanded by Birkbeck Hill as *Johnsonian Miscellanies*. Modern scholarship has gone behind Croker, and even behind Malone; the text of most modern editions follows the third, and contains hardly anything which Boswell did not himself include. But in one form or another the *Life* has always been in print and in demand; and we may say of Boswell what Johnson said of Shakespeare, and Boswell of Johnson, that he 'may now begin to assume the dignity of an ancient'.

Contemporary criticism of Johnson is for the most part anonymous, scurrilous, and nugatory. It was the work of obscure scribblers, inspired by political animus, or Scottish prejudice, or the desire to stand well with some of those great persons whom Johnson had offended. Of these effusions perhaps the least forgotten is *Lexiphanes, a Dialogue. Imitated from Lucian, and suited to the present Times. Being an Attempt to restore the English Tongue to its ancient Purity, and to correct, as well as expose, the affected Style, hard Words, and absurd Phraseology of many late Writers, and particularly of our*

Johnson's Reputation

English Lexiphanes, the Rambler. The writer was one Campbell, 'a purser of a man-of-war, who, as well for the malignancy of his heart as his terrific countenance, was called horrible Campbell'. The censorious purser, during a long voyage, had found himself alone with the *Ramblers*, as Stevenson's hero afterwards found himself alone with the *Athenæum*; and having been 'in a manner obliged to read them', sought his revenge. He is careful not to commit himself to any attack on the sentiments of the *Rambler*; he keeps his guns trained on verbal targets. The faults he finds are two—the use of hard words and the affectation of 'triplets'. The first charge does not come to very much; the parodies of Campbell and the rest are so exaggerated as to be scarcely amusing. 'At his approximation it started like a guilty thing, and ran vagissating along the champain, as if it had been the youthful masculine offspring of a tauro-vaccineal conjunction', reminds no one of the *Rambler* except by prearrangement. In fact, Johnson's excessive use of *rare* words —the abuse of 'big words' is another matter—is only an occasional blemish even of his most formal prose. The second charge is more interesting; for it was very generally preferred and seems to have been forgotten. Modern critics, when they speak of antithetical prose, have in mind the style which Cicero learned from Gorgias and Isocrates, and with which his influence has infected the rhetoric of centuries. Johnson is often, and with justice, accused of excessive indulgence in this kind of symmetry, which balances thoughts and phrases in two equiponderant scales. But the complaint of his contemporaries is directed not against contrasted pairs, but against what they call triplets or triads. 'I told him, I say, that he should not with impunity derogate from my dictatorial importance, remuneratory honours, and accumulation of preparatory knowledge, with the pertness of puerility, the levity of contempt, and the derision of ridicule.' This is *Lexiphanes*. 'I have laboured to refine our language to grammatical purity, and to clear it from colloquial barbarisms, licentious idioms, and irregular combinations.' That is the *Rambler*. The trick, though characteristic, is not in fact distressingly frequent. Yet the charge was made by Horace Walpole—'triple tautology'—and by Vicesimus Knox—'the constant recurrence of sentences in the form of what have been called triplets is disgusting to all readers'. It was repeated by Whately, and approved by De Quincey.[1]

Criticism of this kind left the monument still standing. Throughout the reign of George the Third, Johnson, alive or dead, wielded despotic authority. Goldsmith sometimes disputed his infallibility. 'Sir,' he told Boswell, 'you are for making a monarchy of what should be a republick.' And on another occasion, 'Is he like Burke,' he exclaimed, 'who winds into a subject like a serpent?' Boswell, who quotes these seditious murmurings, thought them no more than momentary ebullitions of envy. He himself loved to display his hero's fame in every light, and there is no reason to suspect him of suppressing unfavourable judgements. The allegiance of Johnson's contemporaries was, in fact, all but unanimous, and almost without reservation. His death

---

[1] Cf. Cobbett, *English Grammar*, Letter 21: '... that *see-saw*, in which Dr. Johnson so much delighted, and which, falling into the hands of novel-writers and Members of Parliament, has, by moving unencumbered with any of the Doctor's reason or sense, lulled so many thousands asleep!'

'made a chasm, which not only nothing can fill up, but which nothing has a tendency to fill up. Johnson is dead. Let us go to the next best: there is nobody—no man can be said to put you in mind of Johnson.'

The deposition of the Dictator was in part a phase of the general revolt against the standards of his age. In part, as Sir Walter Raleigh has said, it was due to no less universal a motive than that self-respect which has dethroned other monarchs of thought. Its principal spokesmen were the Romantic Critics. These literary Jacobins met, as we know, at Mr. Lamb's house on Thursday evenings, for the making and unmaking of reputations; and there Hazlitt tells us that 'the author of the *Rambler* was only tolerated in Boswell's *Life* of him'. What hard sayings passed at these free-thinking gatherings may readily be collected from the writings of the conspirators. Hazlitt found in Johnson the chief exponent of what he called the artificial or pedantic style, in which 'the words are not fitted to the things, but the things to the words'; which 'destroys all force, expression, truth, and character, by arbitrarily confounding the differences of things and reducing everything to the same insipid standard'. De Quincey repeated the old charge of tautology —'certainly Dr. Johnson was the most faulty writer in this kind of inanity that ever has played tricks with language'— and complained that his ideas, even when 'sufficiently discriminated', were 'applied to no real corresponding differences' in the objects described. Coleridge declared that 'his antitheses are almost always verbal only', and that 'sentence after sentence in the *Rambler* may be pointed out to which you cannot attach any definite meaning whatever'. From what seems mere superfluity of naughtiness, he added that 'in his political pamphlets there is more truth of expression than in his other works'.

For this outrageous judgement Coleridge gives a reason which is significant. Johnson's political pamphlets were superior in sincerity 'for the same reason that his conversation is better than his writings in general. He was more excited and in earnest.' A good reason, if it were true; but we know the contrary to be the truth. Johnson, when he 'talked for victory', or on some impulse of contradiction, might say anything; in his writings he always told the truth, and he seldom contemplated truth without emotion. But a reason for the perversion is easily found. Coleridge and his friends were anxious to find good reasons for not reading the *Rambler*; they neither wished, nor if they had wished would have dared, to question the value of Boswell's *Life*, by which, as Coleridge said, 'it is impossible not to be amused'. They reconciled this diversity of taste by the doctrine that Johnson's talk was better than his writing. They did not, however, claim the credit of this discovery, but were willing to believe that it had been made by Burke. Now Burke regarded Johnson with veneration, and had declared that 'his virtues were equal to his transcendent talents'. The recollection of such tributes perhaps caused Coleridge some uneasiness. He was glad, therefore, to be able to call Burke in evidence, as having (as is elsewhere recorded) 'affirmed that Boswell's *Life* was a greater monument to Johnson's fame than all his writings put together'. But mark the skill with which Coleridge uses this testimony. He discounts Burke's 'testimony to Johnson's powers'

Johnson's Reputation

by the facile explanation that Burke was a courtier; 'and, after all, Burke said and wrote more than once that he thought Johnson greater in talking than writing, *and greater in Boswell than in real life*'.

The Romantics had their way. About the year 1825, as we have seen, the publishers and their public concluded that the *Works* of Johnson were no longer necessary to salvation. The *Life* continued to be printed, edited, and supplemented; and a subsidiary literature began to collect around it, of which Macaulay's *Essay* and *Life*, and Carlyle's *Review* are the most famous examples. The paradoxes and exaggerations of Macaulay have been again and again confuted; but the opposition on which they rest, the opposition of Johnson the talker to Johnson the writer, of Boswell's Johnson to the Rambler, is still hardly shaken. We are still invited to admire in the *Life* the rugged good sense, and the terse homely English, which it is assumed cannot be found in the *Works*; and to smile at pedantry and formality in Johnson's writings from which his conversation is supposed to have been free.

These assumptions seem to be partial and misleading. In the first place it is forgotten—in spite of Boswell's insistence—that the graver faults of Johnson's earlier style are hardly to be found in the work of his maturity. His best English is not that of the *Rambler*. Johnson himself is partly responsible for the excessive prominence given to that work in estimating his writings: 'My *Ramblers* are pure wine.' But it should be remembered that for nearly twenty years, during which Johnson enjoyed his pension and his 'throne of felicity', the *Lives of the Poets* were yet unwritten, and

Johnson's Reputation

the *Rambler* was still by far the most considerable of his original works. It was natural that he should stake his reputation upon it, and that his critics should single it out for attack. We are free from this necessity; and it is an axiom that a writer should be judged by his best work. Yet we are so hampered by tradition that even Lord Rosebery, who describes the *Lives* as 'destined to an enduring reputation', feels bound to depreciate their value in consideration of the vices of the *Rambler*, which he never read, and of *Rasselas*, which he read at school.

Again, Johnson's *Life* is more popular than his works, partly because we all prefer anecdote to criticism, the tavern to the closet; but partly also because it is an anthology. It is actually, in no small degree, an anthology of his writings, and contains sentences which are doubtless read with edification and pleasure, but which, if they were read (or left unread) in the pages of the *Rambler*, might be thought to merit the doom of oblivion.

> It is a melancholy consideration that so much of our time is necessarily to be spent upon the care of living, and that we can seldom obtain ease in one respect but by resigning it in another; yet I suppose we are by this dispensation not less happy in the whole than if the spontaneous bounty of Nature poured all that we want into our hands. A few, if they were thus left to themselves, would, perhaps, spend their time in laudable pursuits; but the greater part would prey upon the quiet of each other, or, in the want of other objects, would prey upon themselves. (*Life*, under date 1 June 1762.)

The *Life* has many elements which are more than reflections of the hero's personality. It is a dramatic work of rare brilliance—'a view of literature and literary men in Great Britain for near half a century'—and it infects every reader with its author's irresistible gaiety. In so far, however, as it consists of verbal quotations, it may be considered as an epitome; and this part of it alone can with propriety be contrasted with any other part of Johnson's recorded expression. If we set aside the hypothesis that Boswell has here improved upon his original, a veracious anthology of Johnson could be made by printing the quotations consecutively. What would the result be like?

We suggest that it would bear a surprising resemblance to a wholly distinct anthology that might be culled from the collected works. This alternative selection would not indeed contain 'low words', nor explosions of anger, nor sallies of rudeness. If we except such accidents, there is hardly a sentence of any weight in the *Life* that might not be closely paralleled from the published writings.

The want of human interest is always felt. *Paradise Lost* is one of the books which the reader admires and lays down, and forgets to take up again. None ever wished it longer than it is. Its perusal is a duty rather than a pleasure. We read Milton for instruction, retire harassed and over-burdened, and look elsewhere for recreation; we desert our master, and seek for companions.

As a specimen of Johnson's conversation this extract has only one fault—that it is too consecutive even for Johnson when his blood was up. Punctuate it with suitable interruptions, and prefix a *Sir* or two, and you may fancy yourself in the Mitre Tavern.

To say that Johnson's talk was in an exceptional degree

Johnson's Reputation

like his writing is to repeat what was once a commonplace. Ozias Humphrey declared that 'everything he says is as correct as a second edition'. 'He is a great orator, Sir,' said M'Leod of Ulinish; 'it is musick to hear this man speak.' A man who talks like a book may naturally be expected to talk like his own books; and there is abundant testimony—if it were required—that Johnson did so. Mrs. Thrale thought the *Ramblers* themselves 'expressed in a style so natural to him, and so much like his common mode of conversing', that she was hardly surprised to learn that they were written in haste and without revision. And Fanny Burney, who had been reading the *Life of Cowley*,

> could not help remarking how very like Dr. Johnson is to his writing; and how much the same thing it was to hear or to read him; but that nobody could tell that without coming to Streatham, for his language was generally imagined to be laboured and studied, instead of the mere common flow of his thoughts.

Too much has perhaps been made of the neglect of Johnson's prose, both by those who defend and by those who deplore it. For, after all, how many prose books are there, written before 1800 and not being works of fiction, that have more disinterested readers than the *Life of Pope*? If frequency of printing is a safe test, *Religio Medici* and *Urn-Burial*, a part of the *Spectator* (always the same part), the *Compleat Angler* and the *Natural History of Selborne*, the *Decline and Fall*, Burke on the Revolution, and of course Boswell himself, have some real popularity. But how many, for their mere pleasure or instruction, read the *Tatler*, or the

Johnson's Reputation

Tale of a Tub, or the *Citizen of the World*, or Sir Joshua's *Discourses*, or Hume's *History*, or the *Letters of Junius*?

However this may be, there is now among lovers of literature a disposition to believe that Johnson's works are more worth study than we were taught to suppose. We are no longer prepared without misgiving to discard the *Rambler* as merely pompous, and the *Life of Milton* as merely malignant; to dismiss the criticism of Gray as ineptitude, and the preface to Shakespeare as impertinence. Johnson's best books have only to be read, and read without prejudice, for their truth and beauty to become plain to us, as they were plain to Burke and to Scott. Their reception will be facilitated if we can throw off a tradition of false and invidious distinctions. Johnson is one.

The making of the 'Life of Johnson'[1]

THE story of the disappearance and recovery of Boswell's manuscripts can never be better told than it has been told by their first editor, the late Geoffrey Scott, whose untimely death has lent a new and tragic interest to a romantic tale. But since the edition in which Scott's work is embedded —a brilliant set in brilliants—is accessible only to a few wealthy collectors and the frequenters of a handful of great libraries, the story may be told again. No one, indeed, who has the chance to tell it is likely to forgo that opportunity.

Every one knows the enthusiasm, the industry, the artifice, with which Boswell accumulated written memorials. But the richness and variety of his hoard have hardly been guessed. Now that we know something of the contents of the 'archives at Auchinleck', we need not wonder at Boswell's appointment of three literary executors. He bequeathed 'all my MSS. of my own composition, and all my letters from various persons' to Sir William Forbes, Edmond Malone, and William Johnston Temple, imposing on them the duty of publishing the papers 'for the benefit of my younger children, as they decide; that is to say they are to have a discretionary power to publish more or less'. The familiar story that the executors made no attempt to discharge their office has now been disproved. But there was

---
[1] *T.L.S.* 6 Feb. 1930: review of Vols. 1–6, edited by Geoffrey Scott, of *Private Papers of James Boswell from Malahide Castle.*

no improbability in it. For theirs was, indeed, as Sir William Forbes wrote, 'a task of very considerable delicacy'. Even if the executors were not afraid of what they might find, the mere bulk of the papers might have appalled them. Scott, working at very high pressure, spent a year or more in deciphering the million and a half words which he computed the collection to contain; and even if miscellaneous rough memoranda were neglected, the mass of the residue was huge. We know, however, from the manuscripts themselves, and from letters which have been preserved (though not in this collection), that both Forbes and Malone had enough piety and enough curiosity to face the task. Boswell died in May 1795; in August Sir William described himself as 'busily employed in perusing the whole', and proposed, when he had done, to send the papers to London by the wagon; Malone was to add what he could find in the London house, and ultimately to return everything. The manuscripts seem to contain only two endorsements by Malone, and one by Forbes; but this is enough to show that they did travel from Edinburgh to London; and we know that they went back to Scotland. That they were sent to Temple in Cornwall is unlikely. Temple's diaries for June–October 1795, and January–August 1796 (in which month he died), are extant, and have lately been edited by Mr. Lewis Bettany. If there had been correspondence between Temple and his coexecutors, it is probable that evidence of it would have been found in the diaries, or in the other Temple papers to which Mr. Bettany had access.[1] It may not have seemed worth while to trouble him, for by June 1796

---

[1] I was mistaken. Mr. Bettany pointed out that on 19 July 1796 Temple

The 'Life of Johnson'

Malone had made up his mind that nothing could yet be done; and Forbes (30 June) expressed his approval 'of your idea of our doing nothing in regard to the publication of any of our late much regretted friend's papers at present, but rather to wait till his second son be of an age fit for selecting such of them as may be proper for the public eye'. The terms of the will may have been the reason, or a pretext, for this passing over of Boswell's heir. But in any case Alexander was unlikely to be sympathetic to any project of publication, at least if Johnson were to figure in it. For we know from Sir Walter Scott that Sir Alexander 'thought his father lowered himself by his deferential suit and service to Johnson. He disliked any allusion to the book or to Johnson himself'; and Johnson's portrait by Reynolds was banished to an attic. James Boswell the younger, on the other hand, was a good Johnsonian; his library in London contained a number of Johnson's manuscripts that must have belonged to his father. He may even be described as a Boswellian, for he helped Malone to edit the *Life of Johnson*. He must be assumed to have known all about his father's manuscripts, for he was Malone's intimate. But when the two brothers died in the same year, 1822, nothing had been done; and thereafter the Alexandrine tradition prevailed.

We come now to the legend, first promulgated by Charles Rogers in his *Memoirs of James Boswell*, published in 1874:

> The three persons nominated as literary executors did not meet, and the entire business of the trust was administered by

received 'a long letter' from Forbes on the subject. Temple's diaries show moreover that he and Malone met in July 1795, and that he was in London in October of that year.

The 'Life of Johnson'

Sir William Forbes, Bart., who appointed as his law agent Robert Boswell, writer to the signet, cousin german of the deceased. By that gentleman's advice, Boswell's manuscripts were left to the disposal of his family; and it is believed that the whole were immediately destroyed.

This phrasing, as Scott shrewdly remarked, 'has the ring of an answer from Auchinleck'. The story is untrue, but it is oddly plausible. For though the executors corresponded, it does not appear that they met; and though there was no holocaust, we know there was a fire. The evidence is a footnote by Malone, which appears in the fifth edition of the *Life* (and in that edition only), in which he explains his inability to verify a letter of Johnson to Boswell, 'the original being burned[1] in a mass of papers in Scotland'. Fires, or rumours of fires? There is somewhere extant a letter from Malone to (we think) Euphemia Boswell[2] assuring her that some papers of her father's had not, as she feared, perished by fire, but were safe in London. We might suppose—for we are now in the realm of romantic conjecture—that this Scottish fire was mythical. But it is better to accept the fire, and guess at its motive and its content. It is tempting to believe that the Johnsonian manuscripts—or all that were found—were maliciously, or religiously, committed to the flames. But it is more likely that James Boswell the younger retained the miscellaneous Johnsonian manuscripts, and that Johnson's letters perished from another cause. One of the most notable gaps in the surviving collection is the

---

[1] The late Commander Rupert Gould suggested that *burned* was a misprint for *buried*. I am tempted to believe him.

[2] Yes. See the *Catalogue* of the Boswell Papers by Dr. and Mrs. Pottle, 1931, p. xv.

The 'Life of Johnson'

absence of the letters of Johnson which Boswell had printed from the originals. For of the letters which were known, within a few years of Johnson's death, to have survived, those of which Boswell owned or borrowed the originals have disappeared, the rest are extant. This fact precludes at once the hypothesis that Boswell or his executors returned the originals to their owners and the hypothesis that his son James had them. In either event they must have survived. The simplest explanation is that the originals formed part of the manuscript of the *Life* and perished when—as we shall see—that perished.[1] For there is evidence that Boswell, following the known practice of the age, sent the originals to the printer. If so, they doubtless lay in their places between the leaves of the 'copy', and there they may have lain for a century, until the fatal day of dissolution.

We return to the guardians of the secret, whom we are constrained to admire. Remembering what Boswell's reputation in the nineteenth century was, we cannot resent his family's reluctance to expose his private life 'for the merriment of Macaulay's pupils'. The destruction of the papers would have been easy, irrevocable, and in time forgotten. Their preservation, and their effective seclusion from public gaze, is a masterpiece of family loyalty. The same motive which enjoined suppression forbade annihilation. The papers were not (for the most part) hidden in a garret; though they had, for a century, no commercial value, they remained in that very ebony cabinet which Boswell in-

---

[1] It did not. Later finds at Malahide and Fettercairn have almost closed the tragic gap deplored by Scott. But nearly all the correspondence between Johnson and Boswell is still to seek.

herited from his great-grandmother and devised, under penalties, as an heirloom—a conspicuous depository to which the eye of speculation must always have been directed.

But not even the archives of Auchinleck are irremovable. To Sir Alexander succeeded his son Sir James; and when Sir James died in 1857 his daughters Julia and Emily became his coheiresses. The elder married George Mounsey, a mayor of Carlisle, and resided at Auchinleck. In Mrs. George Mounsey the flame burned steadily.

When Dr. Birkbeck Hill came reverently in search of Boswelliana, he was sent empty away; a rebuff to which that great scholar responded by a footnote of uncommon ferocity. The legend was now firmly established.[1]

At Mrs. Mounsey's death, in 1905, Auchinleck and its contents passed to her nephew, Boswell's sole male descendant, the present Lord Talbot de Malahide; and the ebony cabinet crossed the Irish Channel.

The credit of piercing the gathered gloom of a century is due, we believe, to the editor of Boswell's letters, Professor C. B. Tinker. He it was who first guessed what lay behind the veil and first verified the guess. It is right to recognize magnanimity in Lord Talbot's breach with an inveterate tradition, which has opened the treasury at last. Of the present owner of these manuscripts, who is also the owner of a Johnsonian library second only to Mr. R. B. Adam's, it is enough to say that he deserved his luck and has justi-

---

[1] Not a footnote. See *Johnson Club Papers*, 1899, 55. A Boswell lady had heard of Hill's 'addition' of 'Boswell's, Life of Johnston', and he was careful to respect her spelling.

The 'Life of Johnson'

fied his adventure. Lieutenant-Colonel Ralph Isham—an American citizen but a British officer—was by inheritance well equipped for the quest. Though his family has been for some centuries American, it is of that Northamptonshire stock which is known to all collectors by the 'Isham Reprints' and by the romantic literary discoveries made at Lamport Hall. And Colonel Isham is a *conquistador* on his mother's side also; we understand that his bookplate bears the motto of a maternal ancestor, *Felix audacia*. Finally, the credit of discovering, in 1927, that the author of *Zélide* was able and ready to devote his whole time to the exploration of fresh Boswellian fields is shared, we are told, by Fortune and Mr. Edward Newton.

Johnsonians have long been accustomed to think of Buffalo, New York, as a literary Mecca. They must learn now to think similarly of Long Island. It was in that lovely country and in hospitable New York that Geoffrey Scott (with little help, except what Colonel Isham himself could give) grappled with the ill-digested mass of manuscript, deciphered its erasures and expanded its contractions, sorted and dated its elements, laid down the plan of the *editio princeps*, and in a surprisingly short time prepared a substantial part of it for the press. It is well known that this edition, which will comprise sixteen or eighteen volumes in folio and quarto, is sumptuously produced to the designs of Mr. Bruce Rogers and is very expensive. But the grounds of Colonel Isham's decision are less generally understood. In the first place, it was necessary to illustrate and authenticate the text with full-size facsimiles. This dictated the use of a very large page; and a large page dictates the use of

The 'Life of Johnson'

a large type, if the result is to be readable and comely. Secondly, the plan was for a partial publication of the manuscripts most obviously important and tractable, and for a diplomatic text virtually without comment. This, it was judged, would rather facilitate than obstruct the preparation of the public edition which would certainly be demanded, but of which the compilation must require years of labour. Clearly, however, the production of a larger and more generally accessible first edition would have been prejudicial to the editions for scholars and for the general public which should follow. In any case we ought to be grateful for the early opportunity of inspecting these noble volumes, which Colonel Isham's generosity has placed in several British libraries. Those who have studied that astonishing work recently published by the Oxford University Press, *The Literary Career of James Boswell*, will learn with satisfaction that its author, Professor Pottle of Yale, has obtained the necessary leave of absence and is even now engaged on the completion of Scott's work. His task, however enviable, is not an easy one; but he has shown that he has the learning and the skill to achieve it.

The volumes before us are bewildering in their range. Many readers will be attracted by the gaiety and innocent egoism with which young Boswell narrates his visits to Scottish country houses and his tour of the German Courts. Some will prefer the candour of the correspondence with Zélide, or the engaging absurdities of the oath which Boswell administered to his brother, 'standing upon the old Castle of Auchinleck', or of his 'Inviolable Plan' of conduct which was to be read daily at breakfast. For novelty, and for international *éclat*, that volume must bear the palm which describes the siege of Voltaire at Ferney and of Rousseau at Môtiers, the astonishment of those great philosophers, their final and all but abject capitulation to the irresistible young Goth. The immense letter which Boswell wrote to Temple, describing his interview with Voltaire, is quintessence of Boswell; 'Temple, this is a noble letter', is his conclusion on the eighth folio page. But many will think, as Scott seems to have thought, that the most important and the most fascinating of these volumes is one which is by no means easy reading, and the novelty of which, in so far as it has novelty, is of mainly negative force. *The Making of the Life of Johnson* differs radically in plan from the other volumes. Instead of presenting a homogeneous text, it gives a selective analysis of an intricate textual problem, tracing the growth of the Johnsonian corpus from the first rough jottings through Boswell's fuller notes, his completed journals, his subsequent revision of those journals, and the final manuscript of the *Life*, to the print of the first edition. For no considerable stretch of the *Life* are *all* the original materials available; but enough remains of each class to make clear the nature of Boswell's process from each stage to the next.

At the outset Scott has no difficulty in exploding the legend which sees Boswell as a stenographer. This had a long vogue; and Boswell's notebook is still his inseparable emblem. But the legend was based on misinterpretation of very slight evidence, and can be proved repugnant not only to probability but also to the known facts. If Mrs. Thrale's insinuations have any foundation, the most and

The 'Life of Johnson'

the worst that Boswell ever did was to make a jotting of a conversation, not (in all probability) during its progress, but before the company broke up. Even this he can seldom have been seen to do, or we must have heard all about it. The kind of shorthand of which Boswell once 'boasted'—'a method of my own of writing half words, and leaving out some altogether'—was used not for simultaneous reporting, but for a different purpose.

More, perhaps, than any man of whom we have knowledge, Boswell lived in and for his journal. Experience gave him so little satisfaction in the retrospect, if it were not captured in his journal, that he writes: 'I should live no more than I can record. . . . There is a waste of good if it be not preserved.' He sighs to think that 'the world would not hold the pictures of all the pretty women who have lived in it and gladdened mankind; nor would it hold a register of all the agreeable conversations which have passed'; and so, if life serve the purpose of immediate felicity, 'perhaps that is enough'. But it was not enough; and, insatiable as was his appetite for life, he denied himself rest and shut himself up, lest the stream of record fail to keep up with the stream of experience. In spite of his industry, however, he was always falling short of his ideal of 'journalizing'; again and again, in writing up his journal, he sets down that he is writing so many days or weeks after the event; and very often he adds that he is writing 'from notes'. It was these notes that were written, from day to day (before going to bed, or next morning at latest), in a 'kind of shorthand'. It was his habit to destroy both his earliest jottings and his fuller notes when they had served their purpose; but thousands of them survive which were never used, and, by good fortune, enough survive, which were used, to show how he converted them into the permanent record of his journal. We need not doubt that he could, as he claimed, 'keep the substance and language of any discourse so much in view, that he could give it very completely soon after he had taken it down'.

The second point of major importance which Scott has established is that Boswell's main collections for the *Life of Johnson* are in his journals, and are nowhere else. There are, it is true, many 'papers apart', to which the journal refers; and many of these are Johnsonian. But they were essentially pieces of the journal, and were 'apart' only because they chanced to be written out of sequence, or when the volume was not at hand. The tiny notebook in Mr. Adam's collection has always been reputed the sole survivor of those 'volumes of Dr. Johnson's sayings in quarto and octavo' of which Boswell admitted the possession, when an 'inattentive gentleman' taxed him with folios. It now appears that it was always unique. It is twice referred to, as 'a little book appropriated to Anecdotes of Dr. Johnson', and as 'the little Book of Notes for Dr. Johnson's Life'; and there is no reference to any other such book. The 'volumes in quarto and octavo' were Boswell's London journals.

This fact may have surprising implications. Undoubtedly Boswell must, at a fairly early date, have made some separate collections for a life of Johnson. He made inquiries of various people; he even talked of going to Shrewsbury to seek out Adams. But he knew very well that if he should write the life, the heart of his book could not be hearsay about Johnson's early years, but the authentic documents and, above all, the *ipsissima verba* which would make up his 'Flemish picture'. If, then, he was content to leave the materials for this book in just the state in which he left the materials for all the other books he never wrote—closely woven into the texture of his past life, encumbered with every kind of irrelevant matter—what are we to think? What becomes of the steady purpose, the long self-discipline, the great goal of his endeavour kept always in sight? Scott comes near to discarding this as another Boswell myth. He tells us that, in all Boswell's private musings during Johnson's lifetime, the 'magnum opus' is hardly put in the balance with legal and political ambitions. And he describes as 'very significant' Boswell's reflection when he heard of Johnson's death, 'that there would be considerable expectations from me of Memoirs of my illustrious Freind, but that habits of indolence and dejection of spirit would probably hinder me from laudable exertion'.

It may be thought that Scott here goes too far. The instability and fallibility of Boswell's purposes do not prove that they were not genuinely held. His intention of writing Johnson's life had, as he told the world in an advertisement in the *Tour*, been long known to Johnson and long encouraged by him. It had been declared to his friends, to some of whom the actual journals had been shown. Materials were always accumulating; and to a man in his early forties it might well seem that there would be ample time to arrange them. Moreover, the Hebridean journal was ready (though not quite so ready as he thought) for publication, so soon as Johnson's death should make publication possible.

The 'Life of Johnson'

But when that day came, Boswell's health and spirits were already sapped. In 1780 he had told Erskine he 'was to write Dr. Johnson's life in scenes'. But the journals of the next four years are silent on the subject. Johnson's death found his biographer 'relaxed in melancholy', and induced in him 'one large expanse of stupor' from which the importunities of booksellers and the menace of rivals were hardly sufficient to rouse him. He might well have failed of his purpose; and the story of how he succeeded is the third of the major discoveries which this book announces.

We knew that Edmond Malone deserved the dedication of the *Tour to the Hebrides* and that he helped to 'revise' the *Life*. A pleasant story (which cannot be accurate, though it was told by James Boswell the younger) dated this association from Malone's chancing to see, at the printer's, a sheet of the *Tour*. It now appears that when, in February 1785, Boswell arrived in London to 'set himself down quietly' and put the *Tour* to press, he in fact plunged into dissipation, and nothing was done. At this crisis Boswell and Malone somehow came into collaboration; and thereafter, as Scott shows from the journals, Boswell 'works with Malone, usually at Malone's; and, it appears, never works without Malone'. This, moreover, was no mechanical labour of tidying manuscript and expanding abbreviations; once Boswell 'breakfasted, dined, drank tea and supt with him and sat till near two in the morning. Yet we did not get a great deal winnowed, there was so very much chaff in that portion.' We need not doubt the substantial truth of Boswell's published declaration, that 'the very journal which Dr. Johnson read' was what he gave the world; none the

The 'Life of Johnson'

less, in *Tour*, as in *Life*, there was elaborate revision. No manuscript of the *Tour* has survived;[1] and if it had, we might be none the wiser, for in the revision of the *Life* Malone never seems to have held the pen. His share, therefore, is matter of conjecture. It is known to some of the friends of Professor Nichol Smith that he long since guessed, from hints in Boswell's letters and elsewhere, that Malone's part was far larger than had ever been suspected. Whatever its magnitude, it is certainly under-stated in the dedication of the *Tour* and in the 'advertisement' of the *Life*. It is incredible that this was from want of generosity in Boswell; we must believe, with Scott, that Malone insisted upon self-effacement.

The success of the *Tour*, though it was immediate and great, did not put Boswell in spirits for the far heavier task that now faced him. He sank into deeper despondency. He had already solicited Johnson's friends, and had received valuable 'packets' of letters and anecdotes. But his materials were still in chaos; and in the work of sorting not even Malone could help him except with moral support. On 22 June 1786 he notes, 'Sorted till I was stupefied'; and a few days later he 'sauntered into various Coffee-houses, "seeking rest and finding none" . . . the tears run down my cheeks'. He came to his 'solitary house, drearily, as to a prison'. But he was again 'revived by Malone'; Malone saved him 'from despicable fickleness'. He shut himself up and worked; and after a time, when it comes to 'revision', the old reliance on Malone is fully established, and he works in Malone's company.

[1] Almost all of it has survived.

The 'Life of Johnson'

The ultimate manuscript of the *Life* has all but perished.[1]
Because of its bulk, or its untidiness, or perhaps because it
was in disgrace, it was consigned not to the ebony cabinet
but to an attic, where damp ate to its vitals. At some time,
probably on the voyage to Ireland, a concussion reduced it
to powder, all but a handful of leaves which it was found
possible to salve. The remnant is of great interest. Yet the
loss of the rest is, relatively speaking, a minor calamity,
since the revised journals, of which large sections remain,
are already so close to the first print that we can reconstruct
the final process. And when all is said—when the work of
revision has been traced through its stages—the conclusion
that issues is the altogether welcome conclusion, that there
is no surprising revelation. When Boswell's workshop has
at last been ransacked, the results previously reached by
scholarship are confirmed. We now know for certain—and
that is our great gain—on the one hand that the Boswellian
record was never a verbatim report, and, on the other hand,
that the finished *Life* is substantially the same thing as the
contemporary records. The revision, careful and artful
though it was, appears as an operation of polishing, not as
a structural synthesis. Perhaps the most important, artistically, of all the changes was the purely formal change
which substituted 'Johnson: Sir', &c., for 'He replied that'.
And though Boswell allowed himself much verbal latitude,
there is ample evidence that he rode his fancy on the curb.
In the London journal of 1773, the epic passage of Langton
Testator, the saying attributed to Johnson, 'I wd not let
rascal take my name', is followed by 'I'm not quite sure of

[1] No! A great mass of it is now in the Yale University Library.

The 'Life of Johnson'

this'. It is not in the *Life*. Just before, where Langton inopportunely spoke of the Trinity, Johnson's 'Sir, I'm surprised that a man of your piety' is followed by a blank. But the blank was not filled by conjecture. The *Life* (Hill, ii. 254) has here, 'He told me afterwards'; and the authentication will be found at iv. 216.

The recovery of Boswell's Private Papers should give the *coup de grâce* to two superstitions. The first, already moribund, is the heresy that Boswell was a mere reporter, a satellite, a shadow; that Johnson made Boswell, as it were out of nothing. The second is the more recent, more insidious, heresy that Boswell made Johnson, not indeed out of nothing, but of fibres coarser and commoner than the texture into which his genius wove them. For here, in the mass of Boswell's diaries, we see him performing the daily miracle of preserving Johnson in his habit as he lived. This is a work of selection and a work of art; but it differs from the records daily impressed on the minds of Johnson's other associates—from the vivid pictures which Burke and Reynolds carried with them from his presence—only by being deliberate, written and permanent. There is in the record nothing that was not in the scene recorded. We see Boswell also, in these same diaries, recording other experiences with equal fidelity and often with equal zest. We are still to guess the quality of many of these records, for the publication of Boswell's ordinary journals as such is reserved for later volumes. But we know enough to accept Scott's verdict: 'The Johnson-record flows in and out of the personal Boswell-record and is not different in kind. The vast, bracing difference is the subject-matter.' And again:

The 'Life of Johnson'

If anything can increase our sense of the ascetic veracity of the *Life of Johnson* it is to read the narrative, as most of it was first written, mingled with the patient tale of Boswell's acts and hopes and humiliations, set down for his own solitary view.

It was no part of Scott's plan, in editing this volume, to furnish materials for a commentary. He confined himself, with admirable restraint, to his proper business of illustrating the genesis and structure of the *Life*. Incidentally, some new and precious 'authentic particulars' peep from their hiding-places. But here, once more, the main, reassuring result of his researches is negative; the great commentary of Birkbeck Hill stands almost unshaken: 'On page after page of Boswell's record Dr. Hill's conjectures are verified, his deductions upheld. By a stroke of irony he was denied these papers, a hundred times by his vigilance and intuition he divined what they contain.' It is far too soon to estimate the effect which the recovery and publication of the Malahide papers will exercise upon literary judgements, and in particular upon Johnsonian scholarship. But it is already certain that these volumes will enhance the literary reputations of James Boswell, of Edmond Malone, of George Birkbeck Hill, and of Geoffrey Scott.

Johnson and Poetry[1]

THERE came into my hands a week ago an essay by the Poet Laureate, which it would be impertinence in me to commend. The subject is Poetic Diction,[2] which Dr. Bridges illustrates by an examination of 'Lycidas', 'Adonais', and 'Thyrsis'. In his remarks on 'Lycidas' he naturally glances at Johnson's notorious criticism, which he ascribes to the operation of 'common sense', and 'an unpoetic mind'. I felt, as I read, that this was a challenge which—however unworthy—I could not but take up. If Johnson had an unpoetic mind, I for one should not be here today.

This view of Johnson is, of course, nothing new. In his own day he was accused of blasphemy against Shakespeare; and those of his contemporaries who disliked him, for political or personal reasons, fastened with glee upon those passages in the lives of Milton and of Gray by which, as they imagined, the Lord had delivered him into their hands. In our time, some of his verdicts on Shakespeare and Milton have been unsparingly condemned. The latest writer on Johnson, Mr. Christopher Hollis, though a fervid admirer of his character and of his writings, declares him 'incapable of aesthetic appreciation'. 'The window of beauty was a window through which he could never look.' 'For poetry, in the strict sense of the word, he cared nothing.'

---

[1] Presidential Address to the Johnson Society of Lichfield, Sept. 1928. Published in the *Lichfield Mercury*, 28 Sept. 1928. *Impar congressus Achilli.*
[2] Vol. iii of the *Collected Essays*.

Johnson and Poetry

Hero-worshippers are prone to the mistake of making for their hero extravagant and unnecessary claims. Boswell could not be completely happy unless Johnson were allowed to derive some 'additional lustre' from his knowledge of Greek. Johnson has himself warned us against this error. 'We must confess the faults of our favourite (he has the temerity to write of Shakespeare) to gain credit to our praise of his excellencies.' We are now content to admit that it matters little how much Greek Johnson knew. It is not now necessary to our happiness that we should think Johnson a great poet, nor perhaps even that we should regard him as an exceptionally subtle and discriminating judge of poetic excellence. But if we are asked to believe him 'incapable of aesthetic appreciation' our peace of mind is at an end. For the appreciation of great poetry is not a rare gift. Dr. Bridges in his discussion of 'Lycidas' makes his appeal to the verdict of common men and even of children. ' "Lycidas" has, in spite of the extravagance of its conventions, grown in favour, and firmly holds its claim to be one of the most beautiful of the great masterpieces of English verse.' He rightly dismisses the notion that 'Lycidas' can be admired only by the learned.

It might be urged [he tells us] that with Milton and Shelley who were educated by Hellenic models, and had come by reading and meditation to have panoramic views of history and truth, it was natural to write at that height—their poetic diction may be the spontaneous utterance of their subconscious mind—but that it is nevertheless regrettable because common folk whom they might otherwise delight and instruct cannot understand it. This is a wrong notion. It was not Dr. Johnson's ignorance or deficient education that made him dislike 'Lycidas'.

Johnson and Poetry

It was his unpoetic mind that was at fault, and his taste in music or painting would probably have been at the same level. Moreover children do not resent what they cannot understand in poetry, and they generally have a keener sense for beauty than Dr. Johnson had—indeed, if he would have become again as a little child, he might have liked 'Lycidas' very well.

We know that Dr. Johnson had no ear for music; neither had Charles Lamb. His indifference to painting (which he perhaps humorously exaggerated) may be explained by the same disabilities which forced him to abstain from botany. But note that his blindness and deafness to painting and music are openly and brazenly proclaimed by himself. He does not say, and could not have believed, that his taste in poetry was 'at the same level'. No. If Dr. Bridges is right, then Johnson, in devoting the best years of his life to the study and criticism of poetry, was guilty of a tragic error. He mistook, and misused, his transcendent gifts.

It is now clear that I, and those who think with me, must not pretend to take a dispassionate view of this question. Our affections are engaged. 'Truth will always bear examination', a Scottish lawyer told Johnson. 'Yes, sir, but it is painful to be forced to defend it.... Being angry with one who controverts an opinion which you value, is a necessary consequence of the uneasiness which you feel. Every man who attacks my belief, diminishes in some degree my confidence in it, and therefore makes me uneasy.'

But, unbelievers will perhaps ask, why, in the face of the strong evidence which they adduce, must we insist upon poetic susceptibility as a part of Johnson's character? Why are we not content to admire and revere him as a great

Johnson and Poetry

moralist, a great prose writer, an unchallenged master of practical wisdom? The answer is, I think, that on those terms we might admire Johnson, but could not love him. It is not possible—at this distance of time—to love a man, however great and good, who thinks 'Lycidas' a bad poem, unless we can satisfy ourselves with some explanation of that strange opinion. Dr. Bridges has told us, in effect, that Johnson was a pedant, to whom the vision that is given to children was not given. Has he not proved too much? Could worldly wisdom, however fortified by morality, however illumined by intellectual power, retain that hold upon the hearts of men which Johnson has always had, if his humanity were indeed destitute of that part of human excellence which we call the love of beauty?

Before we approach the problem of Johnson's dealings with Milton, it will be convenient to collect, from his written and oral works, some specimens of his opinions and tastes on poetry. It would be foolish to omit from the inquiry all consideration of his own claims to be esteemed a poet. That he was a great poet will scarcely now be maintained. There are those who think that he wrote one[1] very good poem; and he certainly wrote some lines, which though far below the highest order of poetry, are yet true poetry. I need not remind you of the conclusion of *The Vanity of Human Wishes*. Perhaps Johnson's highest poetic expression was reached in those lines which he furnished as a conclusion to Goldsmith's *Traveller*:

> How small of all that human hearts endure
> That part which kings or laws can cause or cure.

[1] I had overlooked Γνῶθι Σεαυτόν.

Johnson and Poetry

> Still to ourselves in every place consigned
> Our own felicity we make or find.
> With secret course, which no loud storms annoy,
> Glides the smooth current of domestic joy.
> The lifted axe, the agonizing wheel,
> Luke's iron crown, and Damien's bed of steel,
> To men remote from power but rarely known
> Leave reason, faith, and conscience, all our own.

It is remarkable that Johnson was unable to see any great merit in the poets who were his contemporaries in middle and later life, except in Goldsmith. His praise of Gray's *Elegy*, indeed, is generous, and its sincerity will not be doubted. But it is well known that, in certain moods at least, he decried even the *Elegy*, which he once declared had but two good stanzas. He asserted that Dodsley's collection of contemporary poems (which, at the date of the anecdote, already included the *Elegy* and Johnson's own Satires) contained no poem that 'towered above the common mark'. He puzzled Boswell and others by his failure to see anything in such a poet as Mason. It is stranger to us that he could write as coolly as he does of Collins, whom he had known and loved.

But it will not do to infer from this indifference that Johnson cared only for poems of sublime structure or of commanding human interest. We recall his admiration of Goldsmith's descriptive pieces; the subtleties of his sustained analysis of Cowley; his pleasure in Dryden's 'wild and daring sallies of sentiment', in 'the irregular and excessive violence' of Dryden's wit; his delight in 'the most attractive of all ludicrous compositions', *The Rape of the Lock*,

Johnson and Poetry

and his relish of 'the crouded thoughts and stately numbers which dignify the concluding paragraph' of *The Dunciad*.

Boswell was sometimes tempted to think that when Johnson showed insensibility to the beauties of certain versifiers, those beauties were 'too delicate for his robust perceptions'. But he is constrained to add that 'when he took the trouble to analyse critically, he generally convinced us that he was in the right.' His reading of poetry was by common consent 'grand and affecting'. Mrs. Thrale protests that 'it defeats all power of description; but whoever once heard him repeat an ode of Horace would be long before they could endure to hear it repeated by another'. Nor was his appreciation always calmly and placidly critical. 'Such was his sensibility', Boswell tells us, 'and so much was he affected by pathetick poetry, that when he was reading Dr. Beattie's "Hermit" in my presence, it brought tears to his eyes.' When he declaimed against devotional poetry, Mrs. Thrale used to remind him that 'when he would try to repeat the Dies irae, dies illa, he could never pass the stanza ending thus, "Tantus labor non sit cassus", without bursting into a flood of tears'.

Johnson's admiration of Thomson is significant. Thomson wrote about the beauties of Nature (to which Johnson has been supposed indifferent), and in blank verse (which Johnson notoriously disliked). Yet it appears that it was Johnson who secured his admission to the collection of the Poets, from which the Booksellers designed to exclude him. His estimate of Thomson's poetry deserves to be quoted.

He is entitled to one praise of the highest kind; his mode of thinking, and of expressing his thoughts, is original. His blank

Johnson and Poetry

verse is no more the blank verse of Milton than the rhymes of Prior are the rhymes of Cowley. His numbers, his pauses, his diction, are of his own growth, without transcription, without imitation. He thinks in a peculiar train, and he thinks always as a man of genius; he looks round on Nature and Life with the eye which Nature bestows only on a poet; the eye that distinguishes, in everything presented to its view, whatever there is on which imagination can delight to be detained, and with a mind that at once comprehends the vast, and attends to the minute. The reader of the 'Seasons' wonders that he never saw before what Thomson shows him, and that he never yet has felt what Thomson impresses.

I might exclude Shakespeare from this argument, because Shakespeare is so vast, that admiration and love of him may be plausibly ascribed to other attractions than those purely poetical. But I allow myself one illustration. Johnson in discussing Macbeth's famous speech (II. i. 49) on night contrasts it with a parallel in Dryden's *Conquest of Mexico*. This is his note:

Night is described by two great poets, but one describes a night of quiet, the other of perturbation. In the night of Dryden, all the disturbers of the world are laid asleep; in that of Shakespeare, nothing but sorcery, lust, and murder, is awake. He that reads Dryden, finds himself lulled with serenity, and disposed to solitude and contemplation. He that peruses Shakespeare looks round alarmed and starts to find himself alone.

The attitude of Johnson to Milton is a matter of admitted difficulty. If we consider it in the light of Johnson's known prepossessions, we shall remember, on the one side, that Milton was a regicide, and that Johnson moreover disliked him for more than his politics, as a morose and acrimonious

Johnson and Poetry

man; that Johnson was strongly prejudiced against the use, in poetry, of the heathen mythology, especially when mixed with Christian doctrine; and in particular against the pastoral convention. On the other side, when we come to Johnson's praise of *Paradise Lost*, we shall be bound to keep in mind his theological interest and his profound piety. The *Paradise Lost* was a work which he could not but admire, even against his will.

It is worth while to examine in some detail the history of Johnson's relation to Milton. It began early. In 1750, when Johnson was still a young man, and still at heart a Jacobite—when his Toryism was still kept alive by his hatred of George II—he was deluded by a Scottish literary adventurer, one William Lauder, who by an impudent forgery had made it appear that Milton in his *Paradise Lost* had borrowed largely from the work of modern Latinists. Lauder's method was to interpolate, in the poems of Grotius and others, Latin translations of lines from *Paradise Lost*, and to confront the result with Milton's English, in proof of plagiarism. The book is called *An Essay on Milton's Use and Imitation of the Moderns in his Paradise Lost. Things Unattempted yet in Prose or Rhyme*. He dedicated it to the Universities of Oxford and Cambridge, and induced Johnson to contribute a preface. Mark Pattison, in his *Life of Milton*, describes Johnson and Lauder as a 'pair of literary bandits', 'conspiring to stamp out Milton's credit'. Let us hear how Johnson introduces this attempt to public notice.

It is now more than half a century since the 'Paradise Lost', having broke through the cloud with which the unpopularity of its author for a time obscured it, has attracted the general admiration of mankind, who have endeavoured to compensate the error of their neglect, by lavish praises and boundless veneration. There seems to have arisen a contest, among men of genius and literature, who should most advance its honour, or best distinguish its beauties. Among the inquiries, to which the ardour of criticism has naturally given occasion, none is more obscure in itself, or more worthy of rational curiosity, than a retrospection of the progress of this mighty genius, in the construction of his work; a view of the fabric gradually rising, perhaps from small beginnings, till its foundation rests in the centre, and its turrets sparkle in the skies; to trace back the structure, through all its varieties, to the simplicity of its first plan; to find what was first projected, whence the scheme was taken, how it was improved, by what assistance it was executed, and from what stores the materials were collected.

Is this picture the outcome of genuine admiration, or is it a piece of laboured irony? Besides the preface, Johnson supplied also a postscript, soliciting subscriptions in relief of Milton's surviving grand-daughter. He recites the particulars reported of her poverty and continues thus:

That this relation is true, cannot be questioned; but surely the honour of letters, the dignity of sacred poetry, the spirit of the English nation, and the glory of human nature, require that it should be true no longer. In an age in which statues are erected in the honour of this great writer, in which his effigy has been diffused on medals, and his work propagated by translations, and illustrated by commentaries; in an age which, amidst all its vices and all its follies, has not become infamous for want of charity, it may surely be allowed to hope that the living remains of Milton will no longer be suffered to languish in distress. It is yet in the power of a great people to reward the poet whose name they boast, and from their alliance to whose genius they

Johnson and Poetry

claim some kind of superiority to every other nation of the earth; that poet, whose works may possibly be read when every other monument of British greatness shall be obliterated; to reward him, not with pictures or with medals, which, if he sees, he sees with contempt; but with tokens of gratitude which he perhaps may even now consider as not unworthy of the regard of an immortal spirit.

When Lauder's fraud was exposed, Johnson dictated to him a confession and apology, which was printed. 'He saved himself', wrote Pattison, 'by sacrificing his comrade. He afterwards took ample revenge for the mortification of this exposure in his "Lives of the Poets", in which he employed all his vigorous powers and consummate skill to write down Milton.'

Hear some of the terms in which this malignant critic, after waiting thirty years, took at last his mean revenge. These are the words in which he describes the range and scope of *Paradise Lost*:

He seems to have been well acquainted with his own genius, and to know what it was that Nature had bestowed upon him more bountifully than upon others; the power of displaying the vast, illuminating the splendid, enforcing the awful, darkening the gloomy, and aggravating the dreadful. He therefore chose a subject on which too much could not be said, on which he might tire his fancy without the censure of extravagance.

The appearances of nature, and the occurrences of life, did not satiate his appetite of greatness. To paint things as they are, requires a minute attention, and employs the memory rather than the fancy. Milton's delight was to sport in the wide regions of possibility. Reality was a scene too narrow for his mind. He sent his faculties out upon discovery, into worlds where only imagination can travel, and delighted to form new modes of existence, and furnish sentiment and action to superior beings; to trace the counsels of hell, or accompany the choirs of Heaven.

Let it be remembered that the subject of *Paradise Lost*, and the poet's relation to his theme, were sufficient in themselves to command Johnson's respect. 'Every line', he says, 'breathes sanctity of thought and purity of manners.' The end of the poem 'is to raise the thoughts above sublunary cares or pleasures'. Milton's 'studies and meditations were an habitual prayer'. The effect on Johnson's mind may have been so powerful as to silence prejudice and extort praise. But rational, respectful admiration for a great labour of piety does not seem to explain the sentences we have quoted; they ring with the delight, the undying astonishment, that greets poetic greatness. Is it not natural to suppose that the critic enjoyed the poem, was moved to eloquence by its poetical beauties?

When Johnson comes to the discussion of Milton's peculiarity of diction he dismisses the doctrine that it should be imputed to his 'laborious endeavours after words suitable to the grandeur of his idea'.

The truth is that, both in prose and verse, he had formed his stile by a perverse and pedantick principle. He was desirous to use English words with a foreign idiom. This in all his prose is discovered and condemned; for there judgment operates freely, neither softened by the beauty nor awed by the dignity of his thoughts; but such is the power of his poetry, that his call is obeyed without resistance, the reader feels himself in captivity to a higher and a nobler mind, and criticism sinks in admiration.

Is not this language strangely like Dr. Bridges's on a very similar subject? Dr. Bridges tells us that Milton, by poetic magic, so transmutes the pedantic conventions, the 'strange and meaningless' terms of 'Lycidas' into beauty, that they do not 'sound frigid or foolish in the poem'. 'Such is the power of his poetry', writes Johnson, 'that his call is obeyed.'

Johnson recounts briefly what he considers as the faults of *Paradise Lost*, and adds that 'he who can put them in balance with its beauties must be considered not as nice but as dull, as less to be censured for want of candour than pitied for want of sensibility'. These words, again, are strangely like those in which Dr. Bridges condemns their writer for his censure of 'Lycidas'.

One more passage I must quote, familiar though it is, because it has always seemed to me the authentic language of true sensibility:

> His great works were performed under discountenance and in blindness, but difficulties vanished at his touch. He was born for whatever is arduous: and his work is not the greatest of heroick poems, only because it is not the first.

It is not, I believe, a paradox to add that the gravest of Johnson's adverse criticisms of *Paradise Lost* is evidence for me and not against me. He confesses, with rare courage, a failing which cannot be uncommon:

> The want of human interest is always felt. *Paradise Lost* is one of the books which the reader admires and lays down, and forgets to take up again. Its perusal is a duty rather than a pleasure. We read Milton for instruction, retire harassed and overburdened, and look elsewhere for recreation. We desert our master and seek for companions.

Johnson and Poetry

This might be taken strictly to mean that Johnson read *Paradise Lost* as a duty and without pleasure. But this view is incompatible with the general trend of his criticism. I suggest, besides, that his language is not that in which an unpoetical mind confesses the tedium of reading long stretches of solemn blank verse. Johnson's meaning is not that Milton's verse fails to rouse the reader's sensibilities, but that it harasses and strains them.

We have now accumulated a mass of evidence which seems to support the view, commonly accepted, that Johnson was a man of more than ordinary poetic sensibility and power of critical discrimination. This is not a very high claim. We know that men of talents far inferior to Johnson's may, by the exercise of thought and imagination, qualify themselves to receive the pleasure which great poetry gives, and to judge the degrees of poetic merit. I advance a higher claim in urging that Johnson's preferences were strong, that they were independent of prevailing fashion, and that for the most part they were just; we, too, prefer Thomson to Mason, and rank *The Dunciad* above *The Essay on Man*. That Johnson's heart, as well as his head, was engaged in his love of poetry has also been shown; and the variety of his speculations on the instruments of poetry—diction, imagery, versification—proves that his interest in poetry was comprehensive. Finally I suggest that only a true perception, and an exceptionally vivid perception, of the poetic beauties of Milton can be held to have moved Johnson to a strain of eloquence which may itself be called poetical.

It is time to return to 'Lycidas' and the Poet Laureate, and to inquire whether Johnson's failure to admire that poem

Johnson and Poetry

is indeed inexplicable on any other theory than that of sheer inaccessibility to poetic beauty; whether his dislike of 'Lycidas' is enough to upset all probabilities; to nullify the verdict of his age and his own profession; to prove him the victim of a strange self-deception; to convict him of the insensibility which he pitied in others.

The Poet Laureate is, no doubt, familiar with those essays in which Walter Raleigh suggested that Johnson's strictures on 'Lycidas' might admit of excuse, and even of some defence. Raleigh supposed Johnson to have come to 'Lycidas' with strong prepossessions against the use of heathen mythology and the convention of pastoral elegy; prepossessions which may be forgiven if we remember some of the eighteenth-century poems in which Johnson had been nauseated with crooks and pipes, with Delias and Neaeras; and of which it was certainly true that 'where there is fiction, there is no passion'. To this should be added that Johnson was shocked by the mixture, in 'Lycidas', of 'trifling fictions' with 'the most awful and sacred truths, such as ought never to be polluted with such irreverent combinations'.

Raleigh went beyond palliation. 'Is there', he asked, 'nothing artificial and far-fetched about the satyrs and the fauns with cloven heel? . . . Does the beauty and wonder of the poem derive from the allegorical scheme to which Johnson objected?' He went still further in his suggestion that Johnson may be right when he asserts that 'Lycidas' 'is not to be considered as the effusion of real passion; for passion runs not after remote allusions and obscure opinions'. He quotes the poem of Cowley to which Johnson refers, with the remark that:

Johnson and Poetry

there can be no question which of the two poems is the more vivid in its memories and the tenderer in its affection.

> Ye fields of Cambridge, my dear Cambridge, say
> Have ye not seen us walking every day?
> Was there a tree about which did not know
>   The love betwixt us two?
> Henceforth ye gentle trees for ever fade;
> Or your sad branches thicker joyn,
> And into darksome shades combine,
> Dark as the grave wherein my Friend is laid.

And he quotes Johnson's own lines, 'On the Death of Dr. Robert Levett': 'A poor thing, perhaps, to set beside the splendours of "Lycidas"; yet it has in it all that Johnson looked for, half puzzled, in that greater elegy, and looked for in vain. It tells us more of Levett than of Johnson; in "Lycidas" we are told more of Milton than of Edward King.'

Dr. Bridges sweeps these heresies aside. Read the poem, and all difficulties disappear. The heathen deities and the pastoral machinery are properties: and 'in aesthetic no property is absurd that is in keeping'. The properties, like the conventional diction, are right; they are made right by poetic magic. Even that 'strange and meaningless invocation'—

> And O ye dolphins, waft the hapless youth,

'does not sound frigid or foolish in the poem'. The suggestion that 'Lycidas' is deficient in sincerity, Dr. Bridges turns against Milton's critics:

Rather it is evident that it was the very strength of the poet's feelings that has forced the transmutation of his memories and

Johnson and Poetry

of the practical aspects of life into a dreamy, passionate flux, where all is so heightened and inspired that we do not wonder to find embedded therein the clear prophecy of a conspicuous historical event; though the whole of literature can scarcely show any comparable example.

'Rather it is evident.' Any child can feel the poetic magic of 'Lycidas'. And 'though the whole of literature can scarcely show any comparable example', no indulgence is given to Johnson, or to Raleigh, for any failure to feel it.

Between two great critics, I do not presume to decide. Perhaps Dr. Bridges is right, and Johnson is here guilty of unpardonable error. But I suggest again that Dr. Bridges proves too much. If Johnson's condemnation of 'Lycidas' is indefensible, let it not be defended. But it is surely more reasonable to suppose that he erred by some intelligible delusion—or even, if you like, wilfully, by wanton petulance—than to adopt an explanation which, once we accept it, makes shipwreck of his life, of his works, and of his reputation.

If Johnson's response to 'Lycidas' remains, as I think, a perplexing problem, his relation to Milton's poetry as a whole admits of an explanation: an explanation less simple than the Poet Laureate's, but more consonant with Johnson's character. You will remember the unreasonable, but not ignoble, wrath with which old Sir Henry Lee, of Ditchley (in Scott's *Woodstock*), turned his daughter's lover from his house, because that conscientious young Parliamentarian had induced him to express admiration of *Comus*, without disclosing that the poem was by Milton. 'Thou hast made me speak words of praise respecting one whose

Johnson and Poetry

offal should fatten the region kites.' Sir Walter's pleasant fiction may help us to understand what Johnson had to go through. It requires some exercise of the historical imagination to realize how Johnson, in his youth, must have hated Milton; the passions which Milton's life and his political writings must have excited in the young Royalist breast. We are told—and we can believe it—that his 'abhorrence of Milton's political notions was ever strong'. If with this in our minds we read what Johnson wrote, in 1750, of Milton's genius and of his great poem, we shall either dismiss his language as insincere rhetoric, or we shall see in it the rare outcome of a spiritual conflict—the generous surrender which a conquered enemy sometimes pays to his victor. When, in old age, Johnson turned once more to this theme, we find the old animosity and the old enthusiasm still at war in his heart. It is impossible to read his life of Milton without sorrow that so great a man as Johnson found it so hard to forgive. It should be impossible to read his criticism of Milton's poetry without joy for its splendid generosity, without delight in its noble fervour.

The Literature of Landscape Gardening[1]

THE art of landscape gardening, as it was once understood, has long been dead. But it has left innumerable traces on the face of England and many forgotten treatises on library shelves. The popularity of this once-fashionable amusement is now most often inferred from *Mansfield Park*, where, it will be recalled, the improvements projected to be made at Sotherton Court by Mr. Humphrey Repton and those previously executed at 'my friend Smith's place' do not stand alone. Henry Crawford 'had not been of age three months before Everingham was all that it is now. My plan was laid at Westminster—a little altered perhaps at Cambridge, and at one and twenty executed.' The same eye saw how Thornton Lacey, 'from being the mere gentleman's residence, might be raised into a place'—by the removal of a farmyard, the effacement of a blacksmith's shop, and the conversion of the house to front east instead of north. His sister contributes a cottage at Twickenham, which 'being excessively pretty, was soon found necessary to be improved; and for three months we are all dirt and confusion'. Even Mr. Norris's parsonage house was improved by his successor, though perhaps in nothing more ambitious than the substitution for a rough hedgerow of a walk at once convenient and ornamental.

All this was not achieved by taste and genius alone, or

[1] *T.L.S.*, 22 May 1924.

Landscape Gardening

without attention to the rules, which are set forth in many treatises. The bibliography appended by Mrs. Evelyn Cecil to her entertaining *History of Gardening in England* contains some dozen pages of entries for the eighteenth century. Most of these are scientific or practical—as *Paradise Retrieved, or the Method of managing and improving Fruit Trees, with a Treatise on Melons and Cucumbers*; but many deal with landscape gardening as an art, and even as a branch of philosophy. We can trace in these works the rise of the new art from its timid beginnings, the leisurely formulation of its rules while it enjoyed the sunshine of general approbation, and its final reduction to absurdity in the long acrimonious controversies of the dying century.

The return to nature was heralded by mild protests against the formal style introduced in compliment to Belgic William. We do not seem in this country to have accepted the relentless logic of the Dutch, who are said to have eliminated the vegetable ingredient from their parterres, preferring to work in the more docile medium of coloured sands. But we adopted with enthusiasm their system of clipped trees and hedges, which provided rectilinear seclusion embellished with fantastic forms cut in evergreen. The great practitioners in this style were London and Wise, who though not Dutchmen enjoyed King William's patronage. There does not seem to have been any protest against their methods until, in the next reign, the polite journalists ventured some gentle satire. Mr. Pope in the *Guardian* (No. 173, September 1713) directed a pretty wit against vegetable sculpture. He quotes from 'a catalogue of greens to be disposed of by an eminent town gardener':

Landscape Gardening

Adam and Eve in yew; Adam a little shattered by the fall of the tree of knowledge in the great storm; Eve and the serpent very flourishing.

The tower of Babel, not yet finished.

St. George in box; his arm scarce long enough, but will be in a condition to stick the dragon by next April.

A green dragon of the same, with a tail of ground ivy for the present.

N.B.—These two not to be sold separately.

Addison, in one of the most delightful of all his *Spectators* (No. 447, September 1712), had already entered a plea for the modest charms of natural growth. There is in this piece a gentle, pensive melancholy, so that to read it lulls the nerves, as if one were pacing one's own garden. The garden of Addison's dream is what we now call a wild garden, through which 'a little wandering rill' runs 'in the same manner as it would do in an open field, so that it generally passes through banks of violets and primroses, plats of willow, or other plants, that seem to be of its own producing', and in which the birds are encouraged to do their worst, and best. 'I value my garden more for being full of blackbirds than cherries; and very frankly give them fruit for their songs.' A man who writes like this may be expected to be tolerant of intruders, even of gardeners whose tastes differ from his own. But there is perhaps a touch of malice in the comparison between gardeners and poets in their several classes:

I think there are as many kinds of gardening as of poetry. Your makers of parterres and flower-gardens are epigrammatists and sonneteers in this art; contrivers of bowers and grottoes, treillages and cascades, are romance writers. Wise and London

Landscape Gardening

are our heroic poets [and here follows praise of their work at Kensington]. As for myself, you will find, by the account which I have already given you, that my compositions in gardening are altogether after the Pindaric manner, and run into the beautiful wildness of nature, without affecting the nicer elegancies of art.

A revolution so quietly launched was not likely to move fast. Its progress is in fact somewhat obscure. But it was not until twenty years later that the world was ready for Pope to give the death-blow to the old style and its charter of liberties to the new. There is no hesitancy about the *Epistle to the Earl of Burlington*, variously styled *Of Taste* and *Of False Taste*. Its principles, it is true, are not very clearly explained, and its positive precepts not very helpful. But it was enough that Pope had enjoined obedience to nature; that he had laughed at a number of things that were absurd because they were prim, or because they were ostentatious; and that he had done it in lines which English society could not forget:

> His *Gardens* next your Admiration call,
> On ev'ry side you look, behold the Wall!
> No pleasing Intricacies intervene,
> No artful Wildness to perplex the Scene;
> Grove nods at Grove, each Alley has a Brother,
> And half the Platform just reflects the other.

There is perhaps not a treatise on landscape gardening that does not quote, or parapharase, or echo that last couplet. How far Pope was a pioneer is not easy to determine. Walpole, who regarded William Kent as an 'original', the inventor of a new art, yet believed that he owed much to Pope's guidance. But perhaps this did not matter. The essay

Landscape Gardening

Of Taste, though not very explicit, was full of hints; it was easy for those who followed to claim Pope's authority for their rules, whether positive or negative. We are to follow nature. We are to study variety and surprise—'decency to hide', and to 'confuse the bounds'. We are to 'consult the Genius of the Place in all'. Subject to that proviso, we are licensed to divert waters, to raise or to level, to shut out or to open prospects, to add the embellishment of sculpture in its place. We have leave, on the other hand, to make sport of 'vast parterres', or infelicitous feats of engineering or excess of evergreens, or that overweening ambition of grandeur which produces at last 'huge heaps of littleness'. The *Essay* was as useful as the *Art of Poetry*; it was terse, it was quotable, it was not too precise. All sects claimed its countenance.

Two things may be noted. The first is that though Pope does not here use the word 'picturesque', he does use the metaphor which was to exercise a dominating influence over the art: 'The genius of the place'

> *Paints* as you plant, and as you work, *Designs*.

The other is that though Pope does not use the term—which seems to be much later—his subject is what became known as landscape gardening, and concerns every part of an estate that its owner might wish to embellish. The novelty is the extension of decorative art beyond the limits of what had been called a garden. The history of this departure is obscure. The common view is that of Walpole, who traces it to the sunk fence or ha-ha. It is not unimportant to notice that, though in modern times another etymology has been sought for this word, the obvious ex-

Landscape Gardening

planation—'that the common people called them Ha! Ha's! to express their surprise at finding a sudden and unperceived check to their walk'—was universally accepted in the eighteenth century, and is often marked by the point of admiration. However this may be, it is certain that the ha-ha was an important element in the revolution of taste. Walpole believed that not Kent himself, but his predecessor Bridgman, invented the ha-ha, to get rid of walls and to open prospects, but that Kent was the first to see the possibilities thus unfolded. The ha-ha did for Kent what the apple did for Newton; 'he leaped the fence, and saw that all nature was a garden'.

It seems possible that a less picturesque explanation may be more accurate; that the 'simple enchantment' of the sunk fence was rather a consequence than the cause of the general desire which Walpole thus expresses: 'The contiguous ground of the park without the sunk fence was to be harmonized with the lawn within; and the garden in its turn was to be set free from its trim regularity, that it might assort with the wilder country without.' The design is plain. The garden is to be made natural; the park is to be 'improved' and 'polished'; and the two are to blend in harmony:

> Parts answ'ring Parts, shall slide into a Whole.

Clearly there must be some boundary, lest the deer and the cattle trample the flower-beds or invade the house. But a visible, rectilinear boundary would have spoiled the illusion. The sunk fence was the first of a series of innocent deceptions, invented to meet this difficulty. Walpole says 'it ascertained the specific garden'; but we shall see that bolder

Landscape Gardening

theorists found specification abhorrent from nature, and so either abolished the flower garden or confined it to some remote corner where it could be made invisible.

Hitherto we have mentioned only critical or didactic essays. The best historical treatment of the theme was Horace Walpole's *On Modern Gardening*, which was written in 1770, though it did not appear until the publication in 1781 of the last volume of the *Anecdotes of Painting*. It was often reprinted, and in one edition was honoured by a translation, *en face*, by the Duc de Nivernois. The little treatise is a classic in its kind. It has all the worldly good sense we should expect, yet it has enthusiasm, such as befits the Abbot of Strawberry Hill. Walpole was unable to see merit in gardens planted before Kent's time. He contemns all ancient gardeners, from Alcinous[1] to Pliny; and he quotes Sir William Temple's description of 'the perfectest figure of a garden' he ever saw, only to ridicule it. This was the garden at Moor Park, in Hertfordshire, made by that Countess of Bedford who was 'esteemed among the greatest wits of her time, and celebrated by Doctor Donne'. It was of the Italianate kind, planted on the side of a hill, with parterres or terraces, divided into geometrical patterns by stone flights and gravel walks, and adorned with fountains, summer houses, cloisters, grottoes, waterworks, and standard laurels. 'This was Moor Park, when I was acquainted with it, and the sweetest place, I think, that I have seen in my life, either before or since, at home or abroad.' The charm of Sir William's picture makes us grieve for the destruction of these Palladian pleasure grounds, which we

---

[1] In the *Odyssey*.

Landscape Gardening

know we should love in spite of their absurdities; which indeed are perhaps more congruous with modern taste than the Gothic of Strawberry or the 'natural' pomp of Stourhead and Blenheim. But we must show indulgence to the zeal of a pioneer. It will be confessed that Walpole had much to endure.

At Lady Orford's at Piddletown in Dorsetshire, there was, when my brother married, a double enclosure of thirteen gardens, each I suppose not much above an hundred yards square, with an enfilade of correspondent gates; and before you arrived at these, you passed a narrow gut between two stone terrasses, that rose above your head, and which were crowned by a line of pyramidal yews.

We cannot wonder that in these 'preposterous inconveniences' reformers saw nothing but 'want of ideas, of imagination, of taste'. And if we convict the new gardening, as we convict the Gothic revival in architecture, of many faults of ignorance, vandalism, and vainglory, we should remember that both movements, however misdirected, were the expression of a spiritual force which for two centuries had been working in our national life. Landscape gardening is important not because it was the toy of wits and noblemen—however amusing the extravagances which came of that connexion—but because it was a groping after nature, and because it began nearly a century before the date commonly assigned to the romantic revival. *Kubla Khan* and *The Lady of the Lake* are in the direct line of descent from Pope, who made a grotto of 'marbles, spars, gems, ores, and minerals', and from Kent, who planted dead trees in Kensington Gardens. The achievements of the improvers were often puny, and their standards often false. But their

Landscape Gardening

ambitions were large and noble. They aspired to 'realize' the landscapes of Claude and the descriptions of Paradise. Walpole, in a passage of real eloquence, declares that Milton, 'with the prophetic eye of taste', had pointed the way; and marvels that for half a century no one dared follow. He quotes the famous passage:

> Thro' Eden went a river large,
> Nor chang'd his course, but thro' the shaggy hill,
> Pass'd underneath ingulph'd, for God had thrown
> That Mountain as his garden-mould, high rais'd
> Upon the rapid current; which thro' veins
> Of porous earth with kindly thirst updrawn,
> Rose a fresh fountain, and with many a rill
> Water'd the garden.

The opening lines, he says, 'exhibit Stourhead on a more magnificent scale'; and in what follows 'Hagley seems pictured'. The serpentine 'made waters' of Kent and his followers may seem to us not very different from the straight canals which they supplanted. But the eye of enthusiasm saw in them the 'crisped brooks' which

> Rolling on orient pearl and sands of gold
> With mazy error under pendent shades
> Ran nectar, visiting each plant, and fed
> Flow'rs worthy of Paradise, which not nice art
> In beds and curious knots, but nature boon
> Pour'd forth profuse.

Long before Walpole wrote, the new art had formulated rules, and the masters had developed their technique. Kent, believing that 'Nature abhors a straight line'—a doctrine which later drew support from Hogarth's 'line of beauty'—established the serpentine and began the destruction of

Landscape Gardening

avenues which was to continue for a century. He used groups of trees 'to break too uniform or too extensive a lawn'. He exploited his horizon, or if it afforded no prospect 'his taste as an architect could bestow immediate termination'. He began that 'veiling of deformities by screens of plantation' which was known later as 'planting out' a stable or an irrelevant church. All these branches of the art gave occasion for controversy, and for the elaboration of precepts which may be read in the textbooks. Of these the most popular was William Mason's *The English Garden*, which appeared in four books between 1772 and 1782, was often reprinted, and was even, in 1785, republished with a commentary.

Mason's poem is uniformly and delightfully absurd. But it must have been invaluable to amateurs. It is dogmatic, comprehensive, and—in spite of blank verse and elevated diction—a model of lucidity. The leading principles are obedience (of course) to nature, unity of design, and the avoidance of straight lines. If 'yawning crags involve' the Genius of the Scene 'with pale horror', he is to be tactfully planted, so as to be 'awful still, yet not austere'. If

> in some plain
> Of tedious length, say, are his flat limbs laid?
> Thy hand shall lift him from the dreary couch
> Pillowing his head with swelling hillocks green,
> While, all around, a forest-curtain spreads
> In waving folds, and blesses his repose.

The terrain is to be treated as a canvas:

> Take thy plastic spade,
> It is thy pencil; take thy seeds, thy plants,
> They are thy colours.

Landscape Gardening

This ideal, it will be seen, is strictly interpreted. It implies a definite boundary, and the poet, making a virtue of necessity, condemns as vulgar the old ambition of prospect.

> Perchance, some vain fastidious eye
> Shall rove unmindful of surrounding charms,
> And ask for prospect. Stranger! 'tis not here.
> Go seek it on some garish turret's height:
> Seek it on Richmond's or on Windsor's brow.

The 'picturesque' ideal involves, further, the avoidance of irrelevant features. The approximation of the original garden to the wilder scene (beyond the ha-ha), and the 'improvement' of the park by 'polishing', naturally pointed to fusion; till in the end the house became an incident of a forest, and the flower garden, if any, had to be made inconspicuous. Mason places it in some 'secluded glade'. It fares, in short, no better than such buildings as, though indispensable, 'disgust the eye', or than 'the patch'd disjointed choir of some old fane' of which, however, the spire may be allowed to show. On the other hand, a building, if a proper part of landscape, may itself be used as camouflage. A farm may assume the semblance of a Norman castle; an ice-house may be hidden by a 'time-struck abbey'.

This is all very logical. But there was another motive. My lord was easily taught to dislike anything that suggested the limitation of his property, and was willing enough that the eye should rest on nothing not his own. This, we fear, explains the disdain of prospect and the elimination of a church which was uncomfortably close to the mansion. (Miss Bertram speaks of the annoyance of church bells.) It explains, too, why Lancelot Brown—who

Landscape Gardening

had succeeded Kent in this professorship—regularly encircled an estate with a double 'belt' of trees. This avoided the banality of a wall, the purpose of which could not have been mistaken; it often served also to obliterate the surrounding country. This motive was recognized under the heading of 'appropriation', a term employed by Humphrey Repton, the third of the great practitioners. 'The pleasure of appropriation,' he exclaimed, 'is gratified in viewing a landscape which cannot be injured by the malice or bad taste of a neighbouring intruder'; and among intrusions are reckoned not only alien features but also anything which 'looks as if it belonged to another'.

The line of beauty is accepted by Mason as of universal validity. It is

> that peculiar curve,
> Alike averse to crooked and to straight,
> Where sweet Simplicity resides.

But even sweet simplicity must study to avoid repetition and parallelism.

> Vainly Taste
> Draws through the grove her path in easiest bend,
> If, on the margin of its woody rides,
> The measur'd greensward waves in kindred flow:
> Oft let the turf recede, and oft approach.

This, of course, was death to the old avenue and vista, for which, however, prejudice and affection pleaded strongly. Walpole, admitting that an avenue crossing a park or separating a lawn was a capital fault, thought that

A great avenue cut through woods, perhaps before entering a park, has a noble air, and

Landscape Gardening

> Like footmen running before coaches
> To tell the inn what lord approaches,

announces the habitation of some man of distinction.

Mason himself weeps crocodile tears over

> Those spreading oaks that in fraternal files
> Have pair'd for centuries,

and recommends transplantation—a feat actually attempted, though seldom with success.

> But if it fails,
> Thy axe must do its office. Cruel task,
> Yet needful. Trust me, though I bid thee strike,
> Reluctantly I bid thee.

Brown made heroic efforts to compromise, sparing some of the 'monarchs' and making each the centre of a 'clump'; in this way he hoped 'to break the obdurate line'. But later critics of the picturesque school pointed out that the parallels could still be traced.

The nature of the fraud is perhaps best shown in the treatment of fences. A necessary evil, they must be hidden:

> defective still,
> Though hid with happiest art.

They must twist and wind, both because straightness is always and everywhere a vice, and also to heighten the deception. A fence so contrived not merely

> divides
> Yet seems not to divide the shaven lawn,

it does more; it actually promotes the desired confusion. For so

Landscape Gardening

> The wand'ring flocks that browse
> Seem oft to pass their bounds; the dubious eye
> Decides not if they crop the mead or lawn.

But the best lie is spoiled if it may be detected. The sunk fence is useless if it can be enfiladed from a height. Then

> No foliage can conceal, no curve correct
> The deep deformity.

From this dilemma the best escape is to construct a rustic fence of hazels and rope, or to paint the fence green, when

> The barrier pales retire
> Snatch'd, as by magic, from the gazer's view.

Such are the difficulties that beset the painter in landscape; such his methods of evasion. The magnificence of his design rises triumphant above all petty obstructions, and a glowing peroration exhorts the fortunate youth of England to

> Diffuse the blessing wide, till Albion smile
> One ample theatre of sylvan shade.

The work of Mason and his annotators shows the art in the zenith of its prosperity—and, we must add, of its complacency. Scarcely a discordant note had been heard in the chorus of plaudits. Johnson, indeed, was doubtful whether gardening 'demands any great powers of mind'; but even this scepticism he himself ascribes to 'a sullen and surly speculator'; and he generously concedes, for Shenstone's work at the Leasowes, that 'some praise must be allowed by the most supercilious observer to him who does best what such multitudes are contending to do well'.

But the mutterings of revolution were not far distant, and before the century was out the storm had burst. The icono-

Landscape Gardening

clasts who now demand our attention are not concerned with rural embellishment only, but with the whole realm of taste. They followed the speculations which Burke had made fashionable, and were exercised to determine the relation of the sublime to the beautiful and of the beautiful to the picturesque. But they were especially interested in landscape gardening, both for its own sake and because it bore upon this vexed question of the picturesque. That term, from its metaphorical applications, and from its alliance with the romantic, had acquired associations somewhat remote from its etymological significance, and a good deal of confusion resulted. It was generally accepted that the picturesque is rough, the beautiful smooth. But could this convenient distinction be squared with the assumption that the picturesque is anything that can be painted, and nothing else? The Rev. William Gilpin, a pioneer of picturesque travel, hoped that it might, and when confronted, in painting, with unruffled meres and pampered steeds, explained that to the painter's eye these objects are not really smooth at all, but roughened by the impact of light. If an object could not be called rough, he made haste to expel it from the domain of painting—just as, it will be remembered, Catherine Morland 'voluntarily rejected the whole city of Bath, as unworthy to make part of a landscape'. A second champion of the romantic style was Richard Payne Knight, who introduced into *The Landscape, a Poem*, engraved plates showing two aspects of the same house and grounds—the first as nature and the architect had left them, the second as they had been transformed by the improvers. He followed up this attack, at much greater length, in his

Landscape Gardening

Analytical Inquiry into the Principles of Taste. A third member of the school was Sir Uvedale Price, whose *Essays on the Picturesque* grew to three volumes. These gentlemen, in the course of their attempts to fix the principles of taste, and in particular to distinguish the senses in which the term 'picturesque' had been applied or misapplied, and to ascertain its relation to painting on the one hand and to gardening on the other, discovered a good many points of difference among themselves, and this led to cross-criticism in footnotes and appendixes. The popularity of the books shows that even controversy could not exhaust public interest; but it seems to have exhausted Shelley's. 'Do not', he wrote to Peacock, 'let us imitate the great founders of the picturesque, Price and Payne Knight, who, like two ill-trained beagles, began snarling at each other when they could not catch the hare.'

But, however they differed among themselves, the critics were at one in their condemnation of Kent, Brown, and their successors then living. Price declared roundly that the picturesque 'had been totally neglected and despised by professed improvers'; that 'the clumps, the belts, the made water, and the eternal smoothness and sameness of a finished place' could only weary the painter's eye; and that to produce smoothness 'requires neither taste nor invention. He who can make a nice asparagus bed has one of the most essential qualifications of an improver.'

The landscape gardeners took fright. Hitherto they had been well content to be reputed picturesque, and to take credit for 'realizing' the painter's vision. But if the standard of asperity was to be so exacting, it was time to change

Landscape Gardening

ground. Repton accordingly, in the name of the profession, declared that the beautiful, rather than the picturesque, was their aim, and that even convenience deserved consideration. A gentleman's house and garden could not be *all* moss-grown ruins and tangled brushwood. The metaphor from painting was, moreover, misleading. Many beauties of scenery could not be painted: for example, the view from the top of a hill. Besides, the painter stood in one place; his foreground was fixed, and the deer in his middle distance kept their station. But Mr. Repton's clients wished to enjoy the view from the dining-parlour as well as from the drawing-room, and even to walk across it and look back. If they were so devoted to the picturesque as to tolerate a foreground of boulders and brambles immediately in front of the house, it could not accompany them in their walks. Finally, he carried the war into his enemy's country and protested that 'the new system of improving by neglect and accident' was contrary to good sense and to all the proprieties and decencies of a gentleman's place.

All this was very reasonable, and Mr. Repton enlists our sympathy. But if the appeal is to reason, it is plain that the spell is broken, that we have reached the decadence. The routine of improvement went on; some years later, as we know, avenues were still in danger, and Mr. Repton's terms were five guineas a day. But the art had lost its hold upon enthusiasm. Its theorists had made it a part of philosophy. Its practitioners had made it the handmaid of convenience. Shelley waved it aside; Jane Austen smiled at it; Peacock used it as material of farce. Picturesque gardening had ceased to be a theme for poetry.

The Art of Printing[1]

THE age in which we live may claim, in spite of the enormous economic burdens which it sustains, to have witnessed a revival of the arts, and particularly of those arts which may be called democratic. This revival the minor art of typography has shared in a conspicuous degree. Mr. Alfred Pollard, in the current number of the *Library*, passes judgement on the state of book-printing, as it has been exemplified in the exhibition of English and American books, printed in 1923, which was lately arranged by the Bibliographical Society. Mr. Pollard is an exacting critic, but his last word is that 'the trend is still upwards'. The widespread interest in the theory and practice of the art, which is partly the cause and partly the outcome of this improvement, is shown not only by such sumptuous publications as that which is the occasion of this article, but even more by the lively criticism of printing and book-production which is a new feature in literary journalism. The discussions which appear in the *Fleuron*, or in the notes contributed by Mr. Newdigate to the *London Mercury*, are in themselves novel and stimulating; it is more remarkable that a large number of people should wish to read them.

Among these enthusiasts Mr. Stanley Morison is well known, and the appearance of his great collection, illustrating four centuries of printing, has been eagerly expected.

---

[1] *T.L.S.*, 6 Nov. 1924; Review of Stanley Morison's *Four Centuries of Fine Printing*.

The Art of Printing

The usefulness of such a collection will not be doubted. For the study and enjoyment of fine printing are hard to achieve. Very few of us can hope to possess the beautiful early examples which Mr. Morison illustrates. We can study them, no doubt, but we can hardly enjoy them, in public libraries. So we are humbly grateful for facsimiles, with which we may hope to be on more intimate terms. It may, indeed, be suggested that Mr. Morison's facsimiles are no more accessible to the poor man than some of his originals. Even in a library, however, the book will be invaluable as a guide; and it need not be doubted that copies have been bought by printers and publishers, so that many practitioners will have official, if not domestic, access to this treasury.

Yet—let it be confessed—there are drawbacks to the enjoyment even of so beautiful a book as this. It may be worth while to explore the causes of this discontent. There are, in the first place, technical difficulties, a happy solution of which is not always possible. Mr. Morison has decided—perhaps rightly, and no doubt on artistic as well as on economic grounds—to print no descriptive underlines to his plates. Consequently we have not merely to handle a book which measures nearly 19 by 14 inches, and continually to heave it through a right angle to get it sideways; we have also to turn back to the beginning to consult the list of plates. After prolonged experiment we advise the fortunate possessor not to attempt to sit in a chair, or even at a desk, but to place the book open on a large table with the largest paper-knife inserted at the list of plates, and to walk about a good deal, for rest and degustation. Then

The Art of Printing

there is the difficulty of margins. Mr. Morison, of course, realizes their importance—'much of the grandeur of early books is due to the generosity of their margins'; he also realizes, we are glad to note, that the artistic unit of a book is not the page, but the pair of facing pages. He has shown the margins by means of a tinted background—not a beautiful device, though perhaps better than any other. But are they the right margins? The perfect book should be uncut, or—if it be necessary to perfection that the top at least should be gilded—very sparingly trimmed. Unfortunately the generations of binders have been at feud with the printer's ideal, and many of Mr. Morison's specimens give the impression of something like mutilation. We do not complain of this; it could hardly have been avoided. But we are surprised that Mr. Morison, having laid down the true doctrine of facing pages, should so seldom follow it. Again and again he gives us two or more pages from the text of a single book, but only in a very few places does he give us a complete opening. The temptation of variety has been too strong.

But the trouble lies deeper. Our author's theme is 'the development of style in typography', and typography is 'printing from movable pieces of metal'. Why then does he —like other compilers—give us so many facsimiles of title-pages, which in general owe their interest, in a greater or less degree, to something which is not an arrangement of movable types? He gives two reasons: it is convenient to show the title-page 'because of the bibliographical data which it embodies'. Quite so; but only because the plates have no underlines. Mr. Morison seems to have felt the

The Art of Printing

necessity for a better reason, and he takes the plunge: 'In the vast majority of cases it is the title-page which best displays the book's typographical character and presents its most representative page.' Is not this rather like saying that the mounted officer, riding with drawn sword at the head of a body of riflemen, is the most representative file? Certainly he is the most ornamental.

Why is it that books about printing almost always concern themselves rather with the decorations of printing than with the plain print itself? The reason seems to be this: that typography is not primarily a decorative art. The printed page exists, not to be looked at, but to be read. It is therefore not surprising that a gallery of printed pages (or pairs of pages), however beautiful they may be, rapidly becomes tedious. They have neither the beauty nor the variety which is wanted to make such an exhibition attractive. Each specimen gives but a momentary pleasure, and we pass to the next, only to find that it gives less pleasure, because sameness induces satiety. It is true that a succession of (artistically) identical pages may give great and enduring pleasure to the eye, in and through the process of perusal, but that is because the book has been put to its proper and primary use. A book is a thing to be read, and the typographic art has best achieved its purpose, and expressed its beauty, when it has faithfully served the art of the author and seconded the diligence of the reader. But the interest in printing which is mainly focused on secondary decoration is none the less perfectly legitimate. Woodcuts and other ornaments are to many people much more interesting than mere print; they are certainly more at home in a museum

The Art of Printing

or an anthology. Mr. Morison has done right—though not, as we think, for the reason he gives—to vary his collection with the best ornament he could find; and his book, after all, contains enough plain pages to satisfy the most single-minded of typographical students.

The scope of the book is as generous as its dimensions. It is designed to afford a survey of printing in the roman letter, which is the main tradition of Western Europe, between the years 1500 and 1914. (The actual terminus is not 1914, but, for a reason which does not appear, no printer or designer is admitted whose work *began* after that year.) The fifteenth century is excluded—except for sixteen beautiful plates, which serve as a magnificent preface to the text—for the adequate reason that it has been fully discussed and amply illustrated elsewhere. The first section is devoted mainly to the Venetian, Florentine, and Roman printers of the first half of the sixteenth century; the second mainly to the Paris and Lyons printers of the same and a rather later period; in the third we have Froben and a few examples from Germany. The seventeenth century is a blank save for five examples from Paris. The eighteenth is almost a blank until 1750, and no country except France is much illustrated until about 1790, when a large crop of examples appears, French, Spanish, Italian, and English. The nineteenth century is represented by a number of books, French, Swiss, and English. English and American books printed since 1900 close the series. The numbers of books illustrated (by a much larger number of examples) are, for the four complete centuries: sixteenth, 141; seventeenth, 5; eighteenth, 54; nineteenth, 38. It would be almost, though

The Art of Printing

not quite, true to say that Mr. Morison stops at 1580 and begins again in 1790.

This is a selection remarkable for what it includes, and still more for what it omits. It reflects Mr. Morison's taste, with which few critics are likely to find themselves in complete agreement. But he is not afraid to give his reasons. The primacy in printing passed from Italy to Paris soon after 1550, and Italy did not produce another master till Bodoni; the seventeenth century produced nothing of importance, except for a brief renaissance in Paris; English printing is derivative, and negligible, until the times of Baskerville, Bensley, and Bulmer; Spanish printing is negligible (this we infer—Mr. Morison does not say so) except for the work of Ibarra, a contemporary of Bodoni; finally, the archaistic revival headed by William Morris was 'an anachronism'.

Whatever be thought of these opinions, surely it cannot be held that a selection governed by them gives a true version of 'the development of style in typography'. Typography develops, in a great measure, on national lines. What idea of its development in England will be gathered from a book which gives us, for the whole period from Caxton to 1800, one example of 1717, two of 1757 and 1758, one of 1773, and nine between 1790 and 1798? Mr. Morison's exclusions are even more sweeping than his introductory essay would lead us to expect. He there tells us that 'English printers even of the sixteenth century... seldom rose above the commonplace'. We are not sure what 'even' means; it ought to mean, we suppose, that if the sixteenth century is commonplace, the seventeenth is worse. He goes on, how-

The Art of Printing

ever, to say that the early part of the seventeenth century reached 'a fair pitch of craftsmanship', but that this was ruined by the Civil War, and nothing worthy of us was produced until the eighteenth century. But is this true, either positively or relatively? We should have thought that the English books of (say) 1580, and perhaps also those of 1680, were in general better than those of 1630. Is not the first folio Hooker a better book than the first folio Shakespeare? In any case, none of these epochs deserves obliteration. It may be, as Mr. Morison says, that 'the promise of the pretty title-pages of Denham and Bynneman is not fulfilled in the body of their books'. But the printers who set those lovely borders were incapable of producing work without *any* characteristic merit. It is true that the press-work of most Elizabethan books is bad, and they used worn type. But design is more important than accuracy; and though Elizabethan design is untutored, and even licentious, it sometimes threw off the happiest effects. How, in such an age, could it be otherwise? We may see many faults in the work of Elizabethan printers—all the faults that Voltaire saw in Shakespeare. But we are surprised that an English critic should turn a deaf ear to their wood-notes.

When we come to the eighteenth century Mr. Morison gives us ground for hope. 'The development of sound English type-faces,' he tells us, 'brought to our craftsmen the raw material of fine printing'; and he recognizes that 'the beginnings of a style at once national and fine can be discerned in the work of the elder Bowyer'. It is the more disappointing to be put off with a single example of that printer, and with nothing more, save for one book from

The Art of Printing

Strawberry Hill and two by Baskerville, until we reach 1790. We have little indignation on Baskerville's account, who has had as much fame as is necessary; and none on Horace Walpole's, who has had more than he expected. But we sigh for some of the beautiful folios of the age of Queen Anne and George I. Mr. Morison's neglect of these is the more remarkable because of his praise of Bowyer, and because his solitary example of the period—the title-page of Pope's Works, printed in 1717—is to our thinking worth a thousand of the Bensleys and Bulmers who follow. We had hoped for specimens of even finer things; the title-page of Pope's Iliad, also printed by Bowyer, and a flawless example of its kind; the exquisite series of Pope's and Prior's Satires and Epistles; the noble Clarendon printed at Oxford in 1702. We miss all these, and we are bidden admire, in their stead, *The Florist's Directory* (Couchman, 1792); Bensley's *Seasons* (1797), the title-page of which is a mere farrago of types; *The Botanic Garden* (Johnson, 1791); and *Remarks on Cavalry* (Barfield, 1798). But Mr. Morison is serious. 'It is no exaggeration to say that the years 1790–1820 represent the finest period of English typography.' Bensley, Bulmer, Johnson, and Martin were superior to Baskerville; and William Morris, whose intentions were good, 'might have done more had he been less blind to the merits of great printers of the previous generation, Martin, Bulmer, and Bensley'.

These oddities, and a measure of inaccuracy in detail, may charitably be ascribed to inadvertence or preoccupation. But we can forgive eccentricity, and even some carelessness, when there is so much enthusiasm and an achieve-

The Art of Printing

ment on the whole so notable. Mr. Morison has put together, with laborious and skilful discrimination, a great number of very beautiful things. He trusts his instincts, but he is always testing them by the light of reason. He is impatient of mere antiquarianism, and insists that the history of printing should be studied 'not as an end in itself, but as an inspiration towards the typographical task before us'. This is the spirit of the modern revival, and it is the right spirit. It has enabled us to shake off that idolatry of the fifteenth century which, as Mr. Morison sees, made the work of the Kelmscott Press and its imitators 'an anachronism'—the product of a dilettantism remote from the real world, which left the ordinary printer where it found him. Producers of books are now learning to study the tradition of the art as a whole, and to apply its lessons without surrendering their independence.

Mr. Morison sets a lofty standard. The fine printer, he tells us, 'begins where the careful printer has left off'. Fine printing requires 'certain vital gifts of the mind and understanding'. These, added to technical mastery, may produce 'a piece of design'—that is, 'a work expressing logic, consistency, and personality'. It is difficult to quarrel with these pious aspirations, but we suspect that the statement of them conceals certain false assumptions. For why should the 'plain' printer be content to be merely useful, and to produce merely 'a piece of clear printing'? Why should not the plainest print be, in its humble way, pleasing as well as plain? Good type is as cheap as bad, and there is no reason why the cheapest books should not have a beautiful letter and a well-balanced page. The artist-printer, on the other

The Art of Printing

hand, may easily be too conscious of his artistry—too keenly aware of the duty of stamping his personality upon his work. Printing, we have insisted, is not a purely decorative art; experience has shown that the limits within which it can safely employ decoration are very strict, and the first business of even the finest printer is to produce a book which will not interpose itself between the author and his reader. It is all too easy for a fine printer to produce something so fine as to be unreadable; to let it appear that his intention was not to be read, but to be admired. Mr. Morison innocently remarks that a fine book 'is more than "something to read"'. We venture to think that the other side of the truth has more need of emphasis. A prudent printer, though he be designing the finest work of his typographical life, will remember that his first duty is essentially the same which confronts every printer of every book. He has to choose his type (in all likelihood neither new nor of his own designing), to regulate its spacing, to fix the width of his measure and the number of his lines, and to apply the result to the area of his paper. In this process there is, doubtless, infinite room for discrimination; yet how narrow is the convention within which it is applied! And when this is done, the greater part of his work, and that by far the most important, passes from the artist's control and proceeds, not indeed mechanically, yet according to rule. All that remains matter of choice is now accessory and subordinate —title-page, headings and the like, initials and other decoration, if any such are part of the design. A conscious striving after originality, at any stage, is more likely to spoil than to enhance the harmony of the whole. None the less, if the

The Art of Printing

printer's personality be worth expression, it will be found, in the event, to have expressed itself.

We state this doctrine, which is, we believe, necessary to salvation. But there is no occasion to preach at Mr. Morison, or at the eminent modern practitioners whose work he illustrates and extols. The book in which these high matters are propounded is itself a model of dignity and restraint; and not its least pleasant section is the last, which is devoted to the work of modern English and American printers. The English examples, with the exception of two books by private printers, are all drawn from the two great University presses. As Mr. Morison has included a number of books later than 1914, he might, without any real inconsistency, have admitted examples of the books recently designed or supervised by Mr. Francis Meynell. No Englishman, however, is likely to resent the pre-eminence here accorded to two living American printers. The progress made by the American presses in recent years is a very remarkable achievement. But two names stand out, those of Mr. Updike and Mr. Bruce Rogers. Mr. Updike enjoys a high reputation both as an historian of printing and as an executant. The specimens of his work given here will sustain that reputation; and we do not mean to detract from it when we say that Mr. Updike's best work, good as it is, suffers by juxtaposition with the best of Mr. Rogers. Mr. Rogers's name, we believe, will stand very high in the annals of printing. He is very learned, but he is devoid of pedantry. He works in many styles, but all his styles are Rogers. His felicity is equal to his versatility, and in matching his style to his subject he sometimes does more than

The Art of Printing

we had supposed typography could do. His title-page to Thoreau's 'Night and Moonlight' consists of five words, not reckoning the imprint; to be precise, of five words, one initial, and three tiny stars. Mr. Rogers has had the audacity to use a 'shaded' or semi-transparent type, and he has contrived to flood his page with moonshine. We confess we do not know how it is done, but Mr. Rogers has done it. We hope he will print an edition of *A Midsummer-Night's Dream*.

Textual Criticism[1]

THE Art which was once dignified by the style of Critical must now, since criticism has been applied to higher matters, be distinguished as textual criticism. This subordination of title corresponds to a real decline. The art of emendation, once the accomplishment, and often the habitual occupation, of every finished scholar, is now become a minor branch of the study of antiquity. There are more reasons than one for this; but the chief reason is that the harvest, in this field, has been reaped, and little is left for the gleaners. There may be a second crop; but if so, the *novum organum*, which Professor Clark and others are, perhaps, forging in their closets, is not yet to our hands. In the study of modern literature textual criticism, though there have been eminent practitioners, has hardly yet attained the dignity of an art. It was long supposed unnecessary, or necessary only to editors of the early dramatists, whose text offered exceptional problems. When a more general need was felt, it was met by improvisation; either by a hasty adaptation of principles and methods borrowed from classical studies, or, more often, by a rough and not too well-informed application of what was assumed to be common sense. The time has come when we are ready for an *Ars Critica*; and we have scholars capable of supplying the need—scholars who are familiar at once with Bentley on Horace and with Bentley on Milton, with the methods

[1] *T.L.S.*, 11 Dec. 1924.

Textual Criticism

of Porson and Cobet, and with the methods of Malone and Mr. Pollard. Given the equipment, it should not be difficult. For the principles of the art of criticism are like the principles of the art of war. Their application, as Johnson said, 'demands more than humanity possesses', but in themselves they are few, and very simple.

The need for methods and for principles is now often recognized, in these columns as elsewhere. Those who voice this recognition are apt to distinguish two classes of editors: the plodders and the high-flyers: the god-fearing and the god-forsaken: those who stick to their documents, and those who foolishly and wickedly plume themselves on their appreciation of 'intrinsic probability'. This antithesis, in the last statement of it, has no meaning. For editing is the examination of documents in the light of probability. No one can edit a text except from the evidence, which is documentary; and no one is fit to edit a text who is not fit to weigh probabilities, who has not the knowledge and talents that may enable him to examine his witness and determine when he is telling the truth and when he is lying. Those who draw these injurious distinctions perhaps mean no more than this, that the art of emendation begins where the labour of collation ends; and that it is rash, nay insolent, to practise it at an earlier stage, to find a verdict before the evidence has been heard. This is obviously true, though, as we shall see, the metaphor may mislead us. For the collation of independent testimonies, always the duty of classical editors, is the rare and exceptional privilege of editors of printed texts. Far oftener than not, there is nothing to collate; there is, strictly, only one witness; and in that case

Textual Criticism

the verdict *is* his evidence, *mutatis mutandis*; it can be nothing else.

But these theorizers have usually in mind those plays of Shakespeare for which the evidence is multiple. And *there* lies a distinction which is radical, though it is hardly a distinction between cautious editors and rash editors. If it be really true that for certain plays we have two independent and uncontaminated witnesses to the autograph of Shakespeare, then, where they conspire, there is a strong probability that the reading, however surprising, is what Shakespeare wrote, unless it be so common and easy a misreading of manuscript that we can believe them to conspire by accident. This does not often happen, if the original is reasonably legible. It is, we believe, true of the four chief manuscripts of Plato's *Republic*, as reported in Professor Burnet's edition, that though they agree in numerous errors due to familiar confusions of uncial writing, in no place do two of them conspire in an error due to misreading of minuscule; that is to say, there is no place in which we need suppose that two of them conspired in misreading the manuscript from which they were immediately copied. Still, such a coincidence may occur. Two independent scribes, or printers, might read $\Theta EIO\Sigma$ for $O\Sigma IO\Sigma$, or πᾶσι for παισί, or (in one kind of writing) 'dash' for 'clash'. But if the reading in question be not explicable in this way, then the 'conspiring' witnesses, *if* there is no collusion, must in general be presumed to be telling the truth.

But this, if it occurs, is the rarest of happy accidents; establishing as it does a textual certainty only less irrefragable than that afforded by the survival of the autograph

Textual Criticism

itself. Of the vast majority of modern texts the condition is radically different; the evidence is unitary, and it is liable to error. A manuscript was given to a printer, and when printed was destroyed. The only person who can be said to have 'copied' the manuscript is the compositor. That there might be many compositors, of course makes no difference; they did not set the same pieces. Nor does it make any difference, from this point of view, that a corrector of the press compared the proof—if he did so compare it—word for word with the copy. That would not be an independent reading. His verification and the author's revision, if any, no doubt greatly enhance the probability that the print is faithful. But it remains true that the print is unique —there is nothing by which it can be tested—and that it may be wrong.

The fact of error is indisputable; and is not difficult to understand. The probability is always great that a printer, apprehending the general sense of a passage, will produce something which, though wrong, may deceive the author himself. The average author, moreover, when he corrects a proof, is not solely or even primarily concerned to ascertain its fidelity to the manuscript; the manuscript is not sacred to him. He is far more likely to be trying to improve upon it, and in the search for improvement may overlook even absurdity. But a good printer does not often produce absurdity—at least, not patent absurdity. It is his specious guesses that are most likely to elude an author's vigilance.

It is now generally accepted that the first edition of a book is always the most important, and commonly the sole, witness of what the author first committed to the press. It is

Textual Criticism

fortunately not necessary to labour this point; but the reason may be stated. It is of course this: that no ordinary author reads the proof of a reprint—if he reads it at all—so as to satisfy himself that it is faithful. He leaves that to the printer, and contents himself with checking his alterations and additions. He may, no doubt, correct errors of the first edition from memory, or from notes previously made. But apart from this, nothing he can do affects the unique value of the first edition, considered as the sole testimony to what was originally written. This is not to say that later editions can be neglected. The author may intrude at any point, short of the grave, and an editor must take account of such intrusions. But, except in so far as they consist of corrections of printers' errors, they are irrelevant to the primary critical problem, which concerns the relation of print to autograph.

It follows from this that the analogy of classical criticism here deserts us. The editor of an ancient text compares manuscripts, classifying and affiliating, with the object of reconstructing, as nearly as he can, the text of their lost archetype. The manuscripts which he has, and the manuscript which he has not, though they may present widely different problems—if they differ in date and in the character used—are all manuscripts. Further, the extant manuscripts are in some degree independent witnesses to the archetype; for if not, the only purpose of examining them would be to discard all except one. Now, different printed editions of a book, of which (as we have assumed) the unique manuscript perished as soon as it was printed, differ from such manuscripts of an ancient author in two ways that are fundamental. In the first place, they are print; and

Textual Criticism

what happens to print when it is reprinted is not the same as what happens to manuscript when it is printed. Errors in reprint arise from mere carelessness, not from any difficulty of deciphering; and since the printed character differs from that used in manuscript, the confusions due to hasty reading are not always of the same kind. Secondly, different editions are not—with the exception stated above—in any sense independent witnesses. The comparison of editions, therefore, though it may tell us much of printers and their ways, will help us only indirectly to a knowledge of the relation of print to autograph, upon which relation the principles of modern textual criticism must be based.

And here we enter upon a wide tract open to research, great part of which is as yet almost untrodden. The science of bibliography, indeed, has been inaugurated. The ways in which the English printer of the sixteenth and seventeenth centuries dealt with his copy have been ably investigated. The editors of the new Cambridge Shakespeare tell us that they are guided by a large collection of demonstrable misprints, which show them the kind of error to which Shakespeare's manuscripts were exposed. Much has been done in the investigation of handwriting. But it remains true that we still lack such an apparatus as classical scholars have long possessed. We do not yet know with any certainty what letters and combinations of letters are, at different periods and in different scripts, liable to confusion. We do not know how far printers were likely to omit groups of words by the error known as *homoeoteleuton*,[1] to which

---

[1] 'Like ending.' The eye jumps from a word to the same or a similar word just below, and omits what intervenes.

Textual Criticism

copyists, modern as well as ancient, are quite extraordinarily prone. (It was committed in copying this article.) We do not know how far, at different times, proofs were 'corrected' or edited by irresponsible persons in the printing house.

The solution of such problems must be laborious. We have not said that it is worth undertaking. Classical criticism was born of necessity, because the texts current at the Renaissance were so corrupt as to be in many places unintelligible. They cried aloud for correction. We suffer from no such grave inconvenience today. Modern texts, with exceptions relatively few, are far less depraved; and it is not to be expected that the application of even the most highly finished machinery would yield results comparable with those that accrued to the labours of a Bentley. Still, our schools of English are every day turning out editors, as yet very inadequately equipped; and problems of criticism are every day being canvassed. It is worth while to inquire what might be done before we decide that it had better not be attempted.

First, then, there is the writing itself. An editor should know his author's hand, or if none of his manuscripts have survived, then the hands of contemporaries. This duty has, perhaps, not been neglected by recent editors, at least of seventeenth-century books. A still more important study, for criticism in general, is the comparative study of printed books and the manuscripts from which they were printed. The results which might be arrived at thus would be virtually certain; for it should not be difficult to distinguish the printer's blundering and botching from any afterthoughts of the author. Unhappily, manuscripts seldom

Textual Criticism

survive the ordeal of the press. In the aggregate, however, there must be ample material for study, at least from about 1700. We have Pope's Homer. We have the manuscript of published letters—Swift's, Boswell's, Lamb's. Sometimes, by a lucky chance, the proof-sheets themselves survive. It would be worth while to compare the proofs of Johnson's *Life of Pope*, which are in Buffalo, with the beautiful manuscript, which is in New York. Finally, and this is perhaps the most fruitful field, the fallibility of printers might be explored by the accumulation and classification of errors of which the correction is not in doubt. The material for this is inexhaustible; and since anything that is not certain may be discarded, the results would be purely objective. One way would be to examine the lists of errata or 'faults escaped' in a number of books of a chosen period. If by such examination it were found, for instance, that in eighteenth-century printing 'seem' and 'from', 'art' and 'act', 'safely' and 'easily' not only are confused but are very often confused, then we should have a certain knowledge, parallel to the classical scholars' knowledge of what happens to $\theta\epsilon\hat{\iota}os$ and $\H{o}\sigma\iota os$ or to $\dot{\alpha}\gamma\acute{\alpha}\pi\eta$ and $\dot{\alpha}\pi\acute{\alpha}\tau\eta$. (Confusion of 'way' and 'may' is established by the errata to the *Ecclesiastical Polity*; and 'my way of life' should be considered in the light of this.) We should know, within limits, what we may reasonably suspect and what substitutions we may profitably try. These weapons are valid only against the simpler forms of corruption; they will not help us much when the printer has himself resorted to rash conjecture. But they will probably serve to correct many places which have not hitherto been seen to need correction.

Textual Criticism

Quite recently (and since this sermon was committed to writing) Mr. Dover Wilson has made an important step in the direction we have indicated. It seems likely that his article on 'Spellings and Misprints in the Second Quarto of *Hamlet*' may come to be regarded as marking an epoch in these studies. He has laboriously classified the errors of that edition in such a way as to exhibit their graphical origin. He had already shown us what confusions are to be expected, on the assumption that Shakespeare wrote a certain kind of hand; he now proves his rules by marshalling the facts, which seem to be irresistible. Whatever may be the history of the text of *Hamlet*, it is not possible to doubt that such confusions as *time* and *tune*, *arm'd* and *a wind*, *proceede* and *proceded*, *mobled* and *inobled*, are due to misreadings of manuscript which can be accounted for, letter by letter. The study of such divergences, by accumulation and comparison, will furnish a new apparatus; and it will not be applicable to Shakespeare only.

When an editor is dealing with the unique printed representative of a lost original, the discovery and correction of error is his sole critical function. (He has also his own printer to look after, and his own fallibilities; but that is not criticism.) It is his business to detect false witness when detection is possible; and sometimes, if skill and luck hold, to divine the truth that has been hidden. But very often his task is complicated by the later incursions of the author. Of books printed since 1700 this is, no doubt, the normal state. Changes which are, or may be, due to the author must be adopted, at least recorded; and if a 'revised and corrected' edition has been produced under the author's

Textual Criticism

supervison, then that edition must in the main be followed. Yet an editor, having chosen an edition other than the first, is never justified in following it wherever it leads him, short of manifest nonsense. Where his edition differs from the first, his duty is plain. He must decide which of two things is the more probable: that the author made a correction, or that the printer made a mistake. The decision is often doubtful, and may be impossible; but an editor must always ask the question, and must answer it as best he can. This principle has only to be stated for its truth to be apparent, yet in practice it has again and again been neglected.

The comparison of more editions than two is here often helpful. An eighteenth-century book has in its third (and authoritative) edition these words, 'My friend will please to pardon.' The first edition has 'My friend will be pleased to pardon.' The choice is not difficult. It is surely more credible that the printer was in error than that the author thought it worth while to make such a change. But when we find that the second edition has 'will be please', probability is advanced to certainty. It is the sequence so common in texts of which there are more than two editions—truth, corruption, patching.

It remains to estimate the degree to which, in the majority of modern texts, conjectural emendation is necessary or admissible. If we except texts which suffered transmission in manuscript copies, or which from one cause or another were printed without due supervision, it is true that the great majority of modern books are free from very serious corruption. In the last two centuries, at least, authors have in general corrected their own books, and have done so with

Textual Criticism

reasonable diligence. On the other hand, this relative immunity has induced a false security. Very few books are wholly free from corruption; and errors have been repeated, in edition after edition of our most famous books, the detection and rectification of which the editor of a classical text would have regarded as his first duty. It is not creditable to English scholarship that such a book as Boswell's *Life of Johnson* should still be deformed by errors, to remove which no more is required than inspection of the first edition.

The admissibility of emendation depends in large measure upon the general character of the text under consideration. This again is not always appreciated. Yet it should be obvious that, if a reading is suspect, the probability that it is corrupt may be supported by the knowledge that the witness is in general untrustworthy, or outweighed by the knowledge that he is in general truthful. This factor might be called the coefficient of liability to error. It may be estimated by our knowledge of the author and of the conditions under which he worked, and in especial by a consideration of the book that is to be edited. If a book seems to reach a high standard of accuracy, then even a very suspicious passage should be given the benefit of the doubt, unless a corruption may be supposed which might readily be overlooked. If, at the other extreme, it can be established that a text is radically unsound, then it is legitimate to offer conjectures as plausible—though not to obtrude them as certain, or foist them into the text—if there is even slender reason to suspect corruption. In such a case even light-hearted guesses need not be condemned as impertinent.

Textual Criticism

The doctrine so often stated—that conjecture is inadmissible except when the tradition gives manifest nonsense—is, of course, refuted alike by probability and by the facts. Most texts lie between these extremes, and are substantially sound but liable to occasional corruption. The fact that numerous corruptions can be detected in reprints, by reference to the first editions, establishes the fallibility of print in general, and raises a presumption that the first editions themselves are not impeccable; for against the presumably greater diligence of the author we must set the higher probability of initial error in setting type from a manuscript which may have been illegible and confused by erasures and interlineations. The possibility of just emendation is, furthermore, ascertained both by the analogy of classical criticism and by the fact that many conjectures have actually been made in modern texts which have later been verified by reference to an earlier edition or to the author's manuscript.

Emendation, then, is a pleasant, a harmless, and even a useful exercise, if it be conducted with due humility. But it must be remembered that error is stubborn, and will often resist to the last. It is salutary to reflect that there must be, in the literature with which we are familiar, many errors which we not only cannot correct but shall never even suspect.[1] What a printer substitutes for the truth is very often something that will pass for truth. This business of detecting corrupt places and of restoring them

---

[1] A secretary in typing my scribble produced *the second of the seven*. This was critically unassailable, since seven things had been named. But in fact I intended *series*.

Textual Criticism

by conjecture has been, we suggest, unduly evaded by the editors of English books. They have neglected as gratuitous, or shunned as licentious, what they ought to have accepted as part of their routine. But if we encourage our young aspirants to practise this branch of criticism—and they are often less usefully employed—we must see that they do not exaggerate their mission or over-estimate their powers. Many readings may justly be thought corrupt which it is yet impossible to mend; and many passages are obscure or illogical not by corruption of the text, but by the fault of their author. The chances of successful restoration are bright enough to justify endeavour, but they are bounded by inexorable limits of ignorance and darkness. 'Conjectural emendation demands more than humanity possesses.'

Thomas Love Peacock[1]

THE admission to Olympus of Thomas Love Peacock, pre-Victorian poet and novelist, is being celebrated by the issue of a monumental collected edition of his works. Four volumes have been published—judiciously edited, equipped with due bibliographical trappings, beautifully printed and bound—and six more are promised. Publication will be in at least three instalments, so that the incense will curl heavenwards many times and from many altars. We hope that its savour will be grateful to the very exacting epicure who now sits with his peers above the clouds.

There can, I think, be no question of the reality and permanence of Peacock's apotheosis. The recognition is no new thing; no one has just discovered him. Ever since Shelley praised him more than a century ago, he has had readers and admirers. Literary craftsmen and connoisseurs especially have always relished his peculiar dry wit, his profound scholarship, and his admirable style. Among men of letters he has been a kind of oracle. But by degrees his fame spread beyond these exclusive circles, and he became more widely known to discerning lovers of literature. The circumstances of recent times have concurred to swell the chorus of appreciation to a joyous clamour. In England today he has

[1] *Saturday Review of Literature*, 18 Apr. 1925: Review of vols. 2–5 of the Works edited by H. F. B. Brett-Smith and C. E. Jones.

T. L. Peacock

perhaps as many readers as any novelist of equal antiquity, except only Jane Austen and Sir Walter Scott.

This is a notable achievement; for Peacock has many handicaps. In the first place he is a satirist, and his first novel was published in 1816. Most of the institutions he pilloried, and nearly all the persons, are dead and forgotten. Worse still, he is both eccentric and monotonous. If he can be said to have a plot, certainly he has no more than one; and it is doubtful if he has more than one character who really lives. His warmest admirers would admit a difficulty in remembering whether a given episode is in *Headlong Hall* or *Crotchet Castle*, or in distinguishing the wit and wisdom of the Rev. Dr. Opimian from the wit and wisdom of the Rev. Dr. Folliott. For the rest, they are playthings. The cranks are cranks, the spirited young men are spirited, and the pretty girls are pretty. But that is all that can be said of them with any confidence. The conversations too, which fill three-fourths of his pages, are very one-sided affairs. Nearly all the sense, wit, and learning—the rapier thrusts and the sledgehammer blows—are wielded by that reverend gentleman who shares his creator's innumerable prejudices; and many of the dialogues might not unfairly be called tilting at windmills. There are also minor irritations, which by accumulation may become serious. We cannot all be expected to share our author's interest in the fine shades of gastronomy, or his antipathy to paper money, or his enthusiasm for the *Dionysiaca* of the poet Nonnus. But we are never spared these topics of panegyric or invective; and Greek quotations lie everywhere athwart the path.

T. L. Peacock

These obstacles are surmounted by sheer artistic merit. The obvious defects of Peacock's books—the work of an eccentric amateur—do not matter, because their merits are so great. He had all the essential gifts: a keen and powerful intellect, a warm and passionate nature, a vivid perception of beauty. By virtue of these qualities he was a good jester, a good lover, a good hater, and an artist.

All these elements of Peacock's genius may be found in his relation with the poet Shelley. Shelley admired him for his scholarship and his wit, and liked him for other reasons. His strong sense acted on Shelley like a tonic. It was Peacock who prescribed 'three mutton chops, well peppered' in substitution for a diet of tea, bread and butter, and 'a sort of spurious lemonade, made of some powder in a box'. Shelley took the prescription, and its success was 'obvious and immediate'. He took Peacock's prescription for other ills than malnutrition; it would have been well for him if he could have taken them oftener. When Peacock made Scythrop—him of the doleful countenance—the hero of his *Nightmare Abbey*, a gloomy, passionate young man who began with schemes to reform the universe and ended on the brink of suicide because he could not marry two young women at once (and so neither would have him), Shelley was delighted by the joke, and provided the book with a motto out of Ben Jonson. It is doubtful if he would have taken so intimate a joke at any other hand. When he left England, his best letters were written to Peacock. Many years after his death, Peacock sent to *Fraser's Magazine* a long review of Hogg's *Life* and Trelawny's *Recollections*. The importance of these 'Memoirs of Shelley' is recognized. They throw, as we should expect,

T. L. Peacock

a dry light upon the obscure places of Shelley's life. But though the light is dry it is not cold.

To readers unacquainted with Peacock I would recommend that they begin with the *Memoirs*; and I venture to tempt them with an extract, which is so characteristic that I do not apologize for its length.

... Shelley came in, with my hat in his hand. He said, 'Mary tells me, you do not believe that I have had a visit from Williams.' I said, 'I told her there were some improbabilities in the narration.' He said, 'You know Williams of Tremadoc?' I said, 'I do.' He said, 'It was he who was here to-day. He came to tell me of a plot laid by my father and uncle, to entrap me and lock me up. He was in great haste, and could not stop a minute, and I walked with him to Egham.' I said, 'What hat did you wear?' He said, 'This, to be sure.' I said, 'I wish you would put it on.' He put it on, and it went over his face. I said, 'You could not have walked to Egham in that hat.' He said, 'I snatched it up hastily and perhaps I kept it in my hand. I certainly walked with Williams to Egham, and he told me what I have said. You are very sceptical.' I said, 'If you are certain of what you say, my scepticism cannot affect your certainty.' He said, 'It is very hard on a man who has devoted his life to the pursuit of truth, who has made great sacrifices and incurred great sufferings for it, to be treated as a visionary. If I do not know that I saw Williams, how do I know that I see you?' I said, 'An idea may have the force of a sensation; but the oftener a sensation is repeated, the greater is the probability of its origin in reality. You saw me yesterday, and will see me to-morrow.' He said, 'I can see Williams to-morrow if I please. He told me he was stopping at the Turk's Head Coffee-house, in the Strand, and should be there two days. I want to convince you that I am not under a delusion. Will you walk with me to London to-morrow, to see him?' I said, 'I would most willingly do so.' The next morning after an early breakfast we set off on our walk to London. We had got half-way down Egham Hill, when he suddenly turned round, and said to me, 'I do not think we shall find Williams at the Turk's Head.' I said, 'Neither do I.'

The simplest elements of Peacock's satire are to be seen in this story, in which a situation rich in absurdity is drawn with the fewest possible strokes, and is the more telling for this economy. A man without satirical humour might have judged it his duty to admit that Shelley sometimes imagined things; but he could not have had Peacock's pleasure in the incongruities of the scene—the inconvenient hat, the early and inglorious termination of the gallant journey. The mere perception of fraud or absurdity does not issue in satire, unless it is heightened by a gust of temper. A certain intolerance and impatience are necessary to satire; but its quality depends on the satirist's emotional state. The peculiar mild pungency of Peacock's satire is due to its freedom from real bitterness. It is an irascible old man that looks at us from the photograph of Peacock taken in his later years. 'God bless my soul, Sir,' exclaimed the Rev. Dr. Folliott, bursting into the breakfast room at Crotchet Castle, 'I am out of all patience with this march of mind.' And so he was; but his impatience did not interfere with his fundamental, his really imperturbable good humour; it did not spoil his breakfast.

Peacock was a realist and a Tory. He believed in custom and tradition. He disliked the diffusion of education, the growth of democracy, the march of mind. He believed—or liked to pretend that he believed—that our ancestors 'saw true men, when we see false knaves. They saw Milton, and

T. L. Peacock

we see Mr. Sackbut'. Like Dr. Johnson, he held that a man who is not in earnest about his dinner should be suspected of inaccuracy in other matters. Unlike Dr. Johnson, he believed in the efficacy of old wine, judiciously and traditionally accommodated to the progress of a good dinner. 'The current of opinion sets in favour of Hock: but I am for Madeira; I do not fancy Hock till I have laid a substratum of Madeira.' He believed in Greek as 'the alpha and omega of all knowledge', the only key to the temple of the Muses —the Greek of Sophocles' choruses, to be mastered 'constructively, mythologically, and metrically'.

These are tenets which might well supply an entertaining writer; but they would not keep him sweet for a century. The secret of Peacock is not in his whimsies and crotchets, nor in his sturdy politics, nor even in his wit and humour; it lies in his love of beauty, and his love of beauty is romantic. Perhaps, indeed, Realism and Toryism produce their finest effects in literature when they are in some degree irrationalized by a poet's frenzy, a saving grace of moonshine. We may think of Dr. Johnson, who wished to have seen the Great Wall of China ('I am serious, sir!'), and did visit the Hebrides in search of what we should call Romance. Peacock, like Johnson, was a poet, whose inspiration did not flow readily in the channels of versification. He wrote a good deal of verse in his youth, but little of it is remembered or memorable—though the novels are embellished with some rare Bacchanalian songs. But he is always poetical and romantic in his treatment of mountain scenery, and of romantic youths and maidens, and of Greek poetry. He places his puppets in a romantic situation, for the express purpose, as it seems, of making them and it ridiculous. He succeeds; but in the moment of success a spirit of contradiction comes to his rescue, and turns absurdity to beauty. So the topsy-turvy morality of *Maid Marian* is saved from burlesque by its chivalry and the half-lights of the forest; and the satire of *The Misfortunes of Elphin*, for all that its objects are greed, sloth, lust, and drunkenness, is conducted, like *Twelfth Night* and the *Birds* of Aristophanes, in the region of pure comic poetry.

This story, as its admirers know, is the quintessence of Peacock and his highest artistic achievement. It contains the Falstaffian figure of Seithenyn, the incompetent guardian of that ancient breakwater, the ruin of which caused the inundation of Gwaelod, obliterated a principality, and reduced its Prince to a fisherman, but did little disservice to the criminal, who made his escape in an empty wine-barrel and lived to empty many more. Not being burdened with a conscience, Seithenyn retains his magnificent power of potation and ratiocination, which must secure his acquittal in any poetic court; and provides a background against which the more generous virtues of his juniors and betters shine the more conspicuous. They stand out, also, against a superb natural background of sea and mountain; and the exercise of their youthful virtues is painted in pellucid prose. Peacock's descriptive powers, here used with a master's economy, enable him to sketch a scene with surpassing vividness. There are few passages in English literature which equal for pictorial effect the catastrophe of *Elphin*, when at the height of the tempest the neglected rampart is severed, the walls collapse, and the sea rushes in on the

T. L. Peacock

bewildered banqueters. Drunk or sober, they are revealed by the lightning and the flaring beacon—the fuddled warden and his retainers, his lovely daughter, the enamoured prince, the frenzied bard. The innocents, being in a condition to walk, make good their escape along the rampart. The fate of the drunkards is left obscure; but we are allowed to suppose them engulfed, and a delightful surprise is prepared for a later chapter, when the identity of the chief culprit is discovered.

Beside witchcraft of this quality, the mundane prose of Peacock's ordinary manner has a coarser flavour. But even his least romantic symposia, from which the clash of the elements and the primitive passions is excluded, deserve degustation for their wit and polish. It is a dry wine, but well matured; and there are no dregs.

Oliver Goldsmith, 1728(?)–1774[1]

THE date is still in dispute. One of the American critics, whose work is described below, informs us that the evidence is 'complicated and extensive', and 'will be presented elsewhere'. We must hope that, however extensive, it will be found still inconclusive. For nothing could be more characteristic of Goldsmith than that the year of his birth should be doubtful. It is not the kind of fact we should expect him to know himself.

But the present year, whatever its claims to centenary rank, has been signalized by the publication of important additions to our knowledge of Goldsmith. It is with mingled shame and gratitude that we add that these come from America. In Johnsonian studies we still lead, with something in hand; but in the modern study of Goldsmith's life and writings American scholars have almost everything to their credit. Valuable studies of special points have appeared in American monographs and in the columns of *Modern Language Notes* and *Modern Philology*. Miss Katherine Balderston has now followed up her work on Percy's Memoir, and her *Census of Goldsmith's Manuscripts*, with an excellent edition of the letters; and Professor R. S. Crane has added some eighteen essays to the canon, in a book of the highest critical quality. The former book is printed and published

---

[1] *T.L.S.* 8 Nov. 1928: Review of Goldsmith's *Letters* by Katharine C. Balderston and of 'New Essays' attributed to him, and edited, by Ronald S. Crane.

Goldsmith

at Cambridge, England. We accept the implied compliment. But the Chicago printer has produced an equally pretty and accurate book.

Taking a long view, however, even the least reasonable of Irishmen could hardly complain that Goldsmith has been neglected in the country of his adoption. We have had, and have, reprints without number of the two great poems and of the better-known essays. Various collections (of little critical value) appeared in the eighteenth century. Bishop Percy was at pains to collect from Goldsmith's own lips such facts of his life as he could recall; at such pains, indeed, that a quarter of a century elapsed before his memoir appeared in the collected works of 1801. The charming story of these delays has been well told by Miss Balderston. Sir James Prior in 1837 broke new ground, adding documentary evidence for the life, and rectifying the canon of the works. In 1848 John Forster published the first edition of his *Life and Adventures of Oliver Goldsmith*, a work which later he both abridged and expanded. It is a mass of ill-digested material, an odd jumble of citation and comment; but it will always be valuable. In 1885–6 J. O. M. Gibbs produced what is still the best edition of Goldsmith. Austin Dobson refined somewhat on the work of Prior and Forster; but in the last half-century we have not done much more.

We cannot praise too highly the diligence and skill of the American scholars who in recent years have started fresh game. They have found in the possession of Miss Constance Meade (of London, England), a descendant of Bishop Percy, the very collection of documents which her ancestor used for the Memoir. (We tremble when we think how many of Goldsmith's precious scraps have already left this country.) Among them is the original Narrative written by Goldsmith's sister, Mrs. Hodson. Their researches in the numerous periodicals with which Goldsmith was or may have been connected have pointed the way to new and valid criteria by which the mass of Goldsmith's fugitive journalism may be traced and weighed. Professor Crane, with an assured grasp of his method, shows how external evidence may be combined with Goldsmith's habit of quoting himself verbatim, to establish a reasonably certain canon. Nor are we left to guess that these labours will issue in the next collection of the works. Miss Balderston, as we have said, promises us a birthday; and Professor Crane in his preface mentions 'the critical edition now in preparation'. We await it in the confident expectation that it will show tact and elegance in the presentation, as well as skill and diligence in the discovery, of Goldsmith's *adespota*.

Miss Balderston's work adds little of importance to the corpus—all too meagre—of Goldsmith's letters. The hitherto unpublished notes are mere scraps, of no great value in themselves; but we know so little of Goldsmith's life that the smallest scrap is precious. Two letters of importance she is able to place in the series, though not to print. These are manuscripts recently discovered and are not yet available for publication. One of them is Goldsmith's reply to Boswell's famous letter of congratulation on *She Stoops to Conquer*; it will be eagerly awaited. But the great matter is to have the letters assembled from a variety of sources, and to have the texts as Goldsmith wrote them, with his own

Goldsmith

spelling and inattention to grammar and stops. These things are part of the picture.

If the records and relics of Goldsmith the man are still deplorably scanty, the remains of Goldsmith the hack writer are already perhaps too bulky. Professor Crane very candidly allows that his new essays add to the bulk without improving the quality. There are pleasant touches of humour and pathos; but we have had it all before. Goldsmith was right in acknowledging and preserving only a part of his occasional journalism. He was careful, for once, of his literary fame. We are right, too, in leaving nothing undone to restore to our author what he chose to discard. Human curiosity will not rest till it is satisfied, though satisfaction mean repletion. We pile up the works of a writer till they become unmanageable, and we are driven to make our own selection.

Goldsmith's character must remain enigmatical. It was an enigma to his contemporaries and it puzzled himself. But its very oddity made it the subject of speculation by competent and sympathetic judges, and its elements, though they may be difficult to harmonize, are clearly traceable. Boswell's sketch of this 'singular character' has indeed been impugned, and some of its strokes are ill drawn. That Goldsmith 'had sagacity enough to cultivate assiduously the acquaintance of Johnson' is a statement not perhaps malicious but certainly ungenerous, and probably unwarranted. When he adds that 'to me and to many others it appeared that he studiously copied the manner of Johnson', we must be cautious in disbelief; for Boswell is on his guard, and relies on corroboration. But he is perhaps guilty of exaggeration. On another point he has been accused of positive blundering. He tells, as examples of Goldsmith's 'ridiculous excess of envy', how

> When accompanying two beautiful young ladies with their mother on a tour in France, he was seriously angry that more attention was paid to them than to him; and once at the exhibition of the *Fantoccini* in London, when those who sat next him observed with what dexterity a puppet was made to toss a pike, he could not bear that it should have such praise, and exclaimed with some warmth, ' 'Pshaw! I can do it better myself.' He went home with Mr. Burke to supper; and broke his shin by attempting to exhibit to the company how much better he could jump over a stick than the puppets.

Walter Raleigh discounted these and similar anecdotes as mere British failure to understand Irish humour. The solution is plausible, and there is perhaps this of truth in it, that Boswell and others, anatomizing Goldsmith, have fallen into the error of simplification; forgetting that beside 'that hurry of ideas that we often find' in Irishmen there may be a hurry of emotions. Goldsmith may have been amused, and angered, by himself as well as by the young ladies (or their admirers) and by the puppets. But on the whole the theory of British obtuseness must be dismissed as too flimsy to stand up against the evidence. Boswell here is, as before, on his guard; he is aware that the instances he quotes are 'hardly credible'; and note the word 'seriously'. It has, indeed, been maintained that the whole of Boswell's account of Goldsmith is distorted by jealousy. It is suggested that he envied Goldsmith his literary success; or, more subtly, that he was jealous because, in the early days, Goldsmith was of the inner circle and drank tea with Miss Williams.

Goldsmith

We have no right to think thus. It may be doubted if Boswell was jealous of anyone—even of Mrs. Thrale. The notion that Boswell of Auchinleck had anything to fear in competition with 'honest Dr. Goldsmith' must have struck him as absurd. Besides, he was fond of Goldsmith; so that his affections concurred with his instinct for veracity and his love of the curious to put him on the right path. It is clear enough that he made an honest attempt to understand his friend, and it is unlikely that he went far wrong. His story does not rest on his unsupported judgement; it is buttressed by the emphatic testimony of Johnson, whom it cannot be supposed that Boswell misrepresents. Johnson loved Goldsmith dearly, and he ranked his literary gifts very high; higher, perhaps, than they deserve to be ranked. 'Nihil quod tetigit non ornavit.' 'He stands in the first class.' 'Whatever he wrote, he did it better than any other man could do.' He praised even his compilations on subjects of which he was ignorant; his Roman History would 'please again and again'; and his Natural History (though the distinction of horse and cow might exhaust his knowledge) was to be 'as entertaining as a Persian tale'.

Against this background of affectionate praise Johnson's less favourable judgements stand out in high relief. It is instructive to compare his verdict with Boswell's. Goldsmith's vanity, the most obvious of his failings, is not in dispute. But we are not done with the vexed question of his enviousness. The specimens, quoted by Boswell, of which Johnson was the object are not all convincing. The famous exclamations, 'Is he like Burke, who coils into a subject like a serpent?' and 'You are for making a monarchy of what should be a republick', are legitimate protests against Boswell's excess of hero-worship. But it is difficult to defend a spiteful insinuation in the talk of dedications. Johnson (from no wish of ostentation, but led on by Boswell) remarked that he had 'dedicated to the Royal Family all round'. Goldsmith: 'And perhaps, Sir, not one sentence of wit in a whole Dedication.' 'Perhaps not, Sir', was Johnson's noble reply. But Goldsmith's envy was vented on meaner objects. When it was said that 'the man Sterne' had had social engagements for three months, 'And a very dull fellow', was Goldsmith's comment. Johnson is once more Olympian: 'Why, no, Sir.'

When Boswell left London in 1773, having engaged Johnson to follow in a few months' time for their tour, which Goldsmith strangely resented, he called on Goldsmith to take leave. 'The jealousy and envy which, though possessed of many most amiable qualities, he frankly avowed, broke out violently at this interview.' Goldsmith made the same confession on another occasion, and Boswell pleaded that the candour of confession extenuated the fault. But Johnson would not have this. 'Nay, Sir, we must be angry that a man has such a superabundance of an odious quality, that he cannot keep it within his own breast, but it boils over.' At this point Boswell hedges, and professes to think that Goldsmith 'had not more of it than other people have, but only talked of it freely'. It is natural to think that a man who avows envy cannot feel it; for there is no emotion which men more sedulously conceal. But Boswell is self-contradictory in allowing the plea for Goldsmith. The topic was discussed once more after Goldsmith's death. This time

Goldsmith

Boswell again pleaded Goldsmith's avowal of envy as an extenuation (but did not argue that the avowal disproved the reality). Again, Johnson refused to admit the extenuation: 'Sir, you are enforcing the charge.' But he confirmed the fact: 'He talked of it to be sure often enough.'

On the matter of Goldsmith's ignorance Johnson is not less emphatic: 'Sir, he knows nothing; he has made up his mind about nothing.' 'It is amazing how little he knows. He seldom comes where he is not more ignorant than any one else.' Such knowledge as he picked up 'did not settle in his mind; so he could not tell what was in his own books'.

Ignorance, the desire to shine, and that 'hurry of ideas' which Boswell notes as Irish concurred to make Goldsmith 'talk at random'; 'it seemed to be his intention to blurt out whatever was in his mind, and see what would become of it'. The resultant absurdities produced the legend that he 'wrote like an angel and talked like poor Poll'. Johnson himself was guilty of this caricature: 'No man was more foolish when he had not a pen in his hand, or more wise when he had.' Boswell protests that this common notion of the 'inspired ideot' (Walpole's phrase) is a gross exaggeration; admitting that he frequently *was* absurd (while rejecting, as 'too refined', Sir Joshua's theory that he was absurd on purpose), but pointing out that he was equally capable of oral wit and wisdom. Boswell's candour is shown in his quotations from Goldsmith, some of which are as brilliant as any *bon mot* in the *Life*. It would be easy to prove the converse—that Goldsmith with a pen in his hand was often more parrot than angel.

The character of Goldsmith presented by his associates

Goldsmith

is not at variance with that which we may collect from his works. In both, as is natural, those features are most prominent which best lend themselves to caricature; the oddities stand out, rather than the beauties. The letters are not rich in direct self-portraiture, but are everywhere revealing. Writing to his brother Henry in 1759 he gives this account of himself. He was then about thirty:

> Immagine to yourself a pale melancholly visage with two great wrinkles between the eyebrows, with an eye disgustingly severe and a big wig, and you may have a perfect picture of my present appearance. . . . I have passed my days among a number of cool designing beings and have contracted all their suspicious manner. . . . I have contracted an hesitating disagreeable manner of speaking, and a visage that looks ill nature itself, in short I have thought myself into settled melancholy and an utter disgust of all that life brings with it.

The picture is serious and true, for all that it is lit by the humour which Goldsmith could rarely shake off. The premature senility of aspect and mood need hardly be overdrawn. He was never a happy man, and he always seems older than he was; for he was only about thirty-five when he became famous, and some years short of fifty when he died. Throughout his life in London his time, when it was not wasted, was almost all spent in drudgery; no sooner had he earned the means of leisure than he threw them away by his profuseness, and had no choice but to return to his task. He was very ill equipped for this business of daily composition. He had little knowledge, and no great power of reflection. The essays of his early years, the material of which he had to find, or to borrow, are read and affectionately remembered for their glimpses of humour and

Goldsmith

of their author's winning nature. It must be confessed that they have little other merit, except their easy manner. The style itself runs thin. Professor Crane is able to show that an anonymous essay is Goldsmith's, because he was fain to quote himself, repeating the same idea in the same words with a rare and pitiable poverty of invention. No wonder Johnson was impatient; 'Sir, it is amazing how little he knows.' We forgive such poverty less easily than we forgive the plagiarism from others, of which recent criticism has convicted him. But it is impossible to be angry with Goldsmith.

When *The Traveller* and *The Vicar* had made Goldsmith's reputation, and anything with his name had a value for the booksellers, he was glad to give up beating his brains for originality and to employ his facile pen in mere unassuming compilation; 'to make up a work of a decent size that as Squire Richard says would do no harm to nobody'. This confession was prompted by criticism of one of his histories of England, a passage of which (conveyed bodily, it appears, from Smollett) was abused for its Toryism. 'God knows I had no thoughts for or against liberty in my head.' These extensive compilations, the histories of Greece, Rome, England, and Nature, have been long since discarded as notoriously and obviously devoid of authority, and are almost *terra incognita*. Johnson's commendations suggest that the anthologists might find in them a quarry not less rich than *The Bee* or *The Citizen of the World*. It might be that when situation and theme were provided for him Goldsmith's selective fancy would sometimes have free play. In *The History of Animated Nature*, certainly, there are passages of singular charm.

Goldsmith

The paradox of Goldsmith—if we are to seek a paradox—is that his best things are so much better than his dead level that they come with a shock of surprise. Some of his contemporaries were unable to believe him capable of *The Traveller*, and had to suppose that Johnson wrote or improved it. But if allowance is made for the limitations of Goldsmith's genius, and of his circumstances, his inequalities are not inexplicable. He was the last man to write much and maintain a level. Even his letters, spontaneous and delightful as they are, resemble a swift but muddy stream, which ever and again leaps for a moment in a ripple of clear beauty. His essays are smoother, but they are more sluggish. He had no power of speculation, and—except in comedy—but little of construction. His genius is the genius of a poet —comic or tragi-comic. His great gift is for the particular—a picture, an episode, a trait of oddity. It is for these that we forgive *The Vicar* all its absurdities. Even these required prolonged application of his slow and wayward intelligence. It was not for nothing that he 'strolled about the hedges studying jests with a most tragical countenance'; the jests are *She Stoops to Conquer*. When his art rises to a general conception it is always some very simple idea, made beautiful and vivid by the warmth of poetic imagination. 'He was a very great man', was Johnson's final verdict. His best pieces make it still possible for us to understand Johnson's praise, if we cannot quite honestly endorse it. But the degree of his greatness is not what matters most. We may rank his works as we will; but we love the writer as his friends loved him, under compulsion.

Chesterfield's Letters[1]

THE letters of Philip Dormer Stanhope have a long history. As soon as he was dead, Mrs. Eugenia Stanhope sold the copyright of his letters to her husband, his natural son Philip Stanhope, to Dodsley for fifteen hundred guineas. The family intervened, and secured certain deletions; but they seem to have been unable or unwilling to suppress the book, and it appeared in 1774 in two handsome quartos. Before long the librarian of the British Museum, Dr. Matthew Maty, produced the *Miscellaneous Works*, with a memoir, again in two volumes quarto, of which the second contains letters *ad familiares*—the Marquise de Monconseil, Solomon Dayrolles, the Bishop of Waterford, and others. Both these collections were extended by quarto supplements, were frequently reprinted in octavo, and became standard works. A fresh collection, the letters to Arthur Stanhope, was added in 1817. Those to Arthur Stanhope's son, another Philip, Chesterfield's distant kinsman, godson, and heir, were first printed by Lord Carnarvon in 1890. In 1845 the letters then known were edited by yet another Philip Stanhope, the fifth Earl Stanhope, better known to historians as Viscount Mahon; and in 1853, having acquired the manuscript of the *Letters to his Son*, Lord Mahon issued a supplementary volume in which he is believed to have made good the most important at least of the suppressions of the first editors.

The present edition, which includes all these letters and

[1] *T.L.S.* 10 March 1932: Review of the *Letters* edited by Bonamy Dobrée.

adds many more, is the first modern attempt at a complete edition. The six volumes, admirably executed by the King's Printer, contain over 2,500 letters (even Walpole's are not much over 3,000), and of these some 1,400 are now first published. Though the text is in 3,000 pages it is still not complete, for mere 'office' letters are given in brief précis only. But this distinction is doubtlessly rightly drawn. The new letters are mostly from the British Museum and Public Record Office, but Mr. Dobrée has had access also to a number of private collections, though not to Blenheim.

Chesterfield frequently condemns illegibility as a gratuitous breach of good manners; 'every man may certainly write whatever hand he pleases'. In this as in most relations of life his practice conformed to his precept. His letters are models of handwriting, and the text has been little corrupted by misreading. Editorial garbling is another matter; but it does not seem likely that much has been lost. Probably, therefore, Mr. Dobrée's edition has not suffered seriously from his not seeing the manuscript of two very important series—the letters to the son and to the godson. The text seems to be reliable, and we have found few misprints. The classical quotations are sometimes shaky. The documentation is thorough; there is an elaborate introduction, a table of letters, and a full index. Though this is a 'limited' and costly edition, many libraries will find it indispensable.

Chesterfield is more famous as a teacher of deportment than as a statesman, and the letters to his son will always find more readers than the letters to his political associates. Yet these dissertations on the art of life are so uniform, they

Chesterfield

have so little of the particular, that they admit of little comment. It is significant that, though Mr. Dobrée's interests are literary rather than political, his long introduction is predominantly a political biography. He describes himself as a layman 'occasionally and spasmodically interested in history'. This, then, has been a long spasm; and Sir Richard Lodge has helped him to keep going. A lay reader's impression is that the introduction and historical notes will be found valuable by historians; at least they are eminently readable.

For most of us it is not the Lord Lieutenant or the Secretary of State who still challenges curiosity, but the man—the wit, the exquisite, the stoic, perhaps the cynic. Like his grandfather, the great Marquess Halifax, he is a character not easily read. There is no doubt that he had great and varied talents, and the will to direct them. But he had no enthusiasm, and perhaps nothing that should be called genius. His letters show none. They are always good, and far above the average of an age in which many men, and not a few women, wrote excellent letters. But they are never among the best. He writes once, in terms conventional but true, that 'letters should be familiar conversations between absent friends'. Now the best letters give something of the effect of familiar conversation, even when one side only of a correspondence is preserved. But Chesterfield's letters have not that trick of genius; they hold no mirror to his friends' features. This is not to call them egotistical. They vary in tone and subject, as letters should, with the correspondent. But they have no dramatic virtue; they make no old friendship live again.

Chesterfield

Not only did Chesterfield lack genius; one is tempted to think that he did not know what genius is. For his belief in the universal adequacy of good sense and formal elegance, with an iron resolution to achieve them, seems to have been incorrigible. He had no humour, and no recognition of humour. He hated laughter—'there is nothing so illiberal, and so ill-bred, as audible laughter'. The memory wanders wistfully to another Londoner, whose decorum was not proof against the absurdity of a friend's making a foolish will; who 'in order to support himself, laid hold of one of the posts at the side of the foot pavement, and sent forth peals so loud, that in the silence of the night his voice seemed to resound from Temple-bar to Fleet-ditch'.[1] Chesterfield had no pity for indolence, and did not conceive that any rational being could 'squander away in absolute idleness one single minute of that small portion of time which is allotted us in this world'. This vice he especially reprobated in the young: 'inaction at your age is unpardonable'. His greatest powers, in his own opinion, and by general consent, were shown in oratory. Yet he insists that if the matter of a speech is good sense, diction and elocution will do all that oratory can do. Doubtless his model was Cicero rather than Demosthenes; yet even Cicero had passion, though this Ciceronian could not feel it. When his godson was eight years old he thought him old enough to be shown the Tower and Westminster Abbey, and so learn *nil admirari*. There is no romance in this rule of life.

The publication of the letters to his son, on which Chesterfield's fame now chiefly rests, was a shrewd stroke

[1] See Boswell's *Life of Johnson*, 10 May 1773.

Chesterfield

to his contemporary reputation. The case against him can be briefly stated; he was accused of condoning, and even of inculcating, deceit and adultery. The two charges are not of equal weight. Chesterfield expresses abhorrence of lying, and was no doubt a truthful man. It was forgotten that he was a diplomatist, training a young man for diplomacy, and that his own careful distinction between simulation and dissimulation is just. Boswell's 'glossy duplicity' may be dismissed as caricature. The other question is more difficult. Mr. Dobrée stoutly defends his hero; and up to a point his defence is good. Chesterfield assumed, as doubtless most men in his situation would have assumed, that a young man at large in continental capitals would allow himself the usual indulgences. On that basis his father's counsel, to shun the lower forms of debauchery, was and is, as Mr. Dobrée insists, good counsel. The positive side of the doctrine is less easily justified. Chesterfield came to believe that the young man's *gaucherie* could only be cured by an *arrangement*, by such deft feminine handling as had polished and promoted Richelieu and Marlborough. This 'desperate remedy', as his first biographer calls it, is often advocated; nowhere, perhaps, more bluntly than in a letter of 30 June 1751, when Philip was nineteen:

I had much rather that you were passionately in love with some determined coquette of fashion (who would lead you a dance, fashion, supple and polish you), than that you knew all Plato and Aristotle by heart.

Here, apart from morals, there is a question of good taste. As Mr. Dobrée remarks 'there are certain intimacies from which some prefer to exclude their fathers'; and we may

Chesterfield

add that the letters to young Lord Huntingdon, when they touch on these topics—as they do very often—show a solicitude for that young man's health and happiness which, though perfectly sincere, is mixed with a rather unpleasing curiosity.

It is to Chesterfield's credit that he has earned the respect and affection of his editors. Lord Carnarvon, who began his task 'with little interest, perhaps with prejudice, ended it with strong interest, sympathy, and appreciation'. Mr. Dobrée, whose drudgery has been more severe, is a wholehearted apologist. He is 'tempted to say that every child should, at some period of his life, sit at the feet of Lord Chesterfield'.

But it will not do to dismiss the general opinion as if it were the voice of Victorian squeamishness, or as if Johnson's famous epigram expressed his personal pique or political animus. Even the official biographer attempts no defence—'we shall content ourselves with deploring the weakness of human nature'—though he pleads that the letters ought not to have been exposed to the public eye. It is in truth not easy to do them justice. It is difficult always to bear in mind that they were written for the sole edification of a boy, who, in the writer's judgement, had a good disposition, good parts, and no manners. If we allow ourselves to think of them as a series of essays—and the illusion is often all but complete—we are bound to find their repetitions, their endless insistence on the minor virtues, intolerably fatiguing. But the alternative is worse. If we allow ourselves to remember that they were letters, punctually delivered, and had to be read—not indeed in bulk, but at very frequent

Chesterfield

intervals—our compassion for the young man, the rather stolid, unresponsive young man, who had to go through the form, at least, of digesting and answering them, may easily drive us to think harshly of the writer. What was poor Philip to make of a tender parent whose letters too often began like this:

> My dear Friend,—In all systems whatsoever, whether of religion, government, morals, &c., perfection is the object always proposed, though possibly unattainable; hitherto, at least, certainly unattained. However, those who aim carefully at the mark itself, will unquestionably come nearer to it than those who, from despair, negligence, or indolence, leave to chance the work of skill. The maxim holds equally true in common life; those who aim at perfection will come infinitely nearer to it than those desponding or indolent spirits, who foolishly say to themselves—Nobody is perfect; perfection is unattainable; to attempt it is chimerical; I shall do as well as others; why then should I give myself trouble to be what I never can, and what, according to the common course of things, I need not be—*perfect*?

But it is indeed our pity that Chesterfield deserves, though he would have rejected the offer. And though the letters had no artistic intention, and show many faults of artistry, their pathos gives them, in some degree, the dignity of a work of art. This was no 'familiar correspondence between absent friends'. Chesterfield's letters are not affected by those he received, which we guess to have been infrequent and perfunctory; there is no interplay; the letters are, indeed, hardly addressed to a real young man, but to a pattern of docility—*cet autre moi-même*—which the writer had fashioned out of his own ambitious and passionate affection, and in which at last he could not himself believe. The more

Chesterfield

'frivolous' the letters become, the more they insist on the graces—*une certaine douceur, l'aimable, je ne sais quoi*—on *décrottage*, and the *arrangements* necessary to that process—the more urgent, the more single-minded, the more strident is their tone. He kept it up, so long as any hope remained; but we can see behind the smooth mask the contortions of bitter and almost hopeless disappointment.

It cannot be pretended that these 3,000 pages are easy reading. But taken in moderate doses the letters have a pleasant astringent quality. They do not sparkle with quotable phrases, but they have always something to say. Even the political letters are readable; and the late letters to personal friends, full of shrewd and witty comment on Vanity Fair, draw a very attractive picture of a lettered recluse, ageing and often ill, disappointed and perhaps embittered, but indomitable, and never wholly selfish.

I am here in my hermitage, very deaf, and consequently alone. I read as much as my eyes will let me, and I walk and ride as often as the worst weather I ever knew will allow me. *D'ailleurs*, good health, natural good spirits, some philosophy, and long experience of the world, make me much less dejected and melancholy than most people in my situation would be, or than I should have been myself some years ago. I comfort myself with the reflexion, that I did not lose the power, till after I had very nearly lost the desire, of hearing. I have been long and voluntarily deaf to the voice of ambition, and to the noise of business, so that I lose nothing upon that head; and when I consider how much of my life is past, and how little of it, according to the course of Nature, remains, I can almost persuade myself that I am no loser at all. By all this, you see that I am neither a dejected nor a sour deaf man.

Chesterfield

When Chesterfield withdrew himself from affairs, resigning the applause of society and the allurements of deep play, he was over fifty and had more than twenty years to live. His constitution was already, in his own opinion, irreparably shattered, and his deafness soon shut him off from the world—'all places are alike to me, as I carry my own solitude with me'—and left him to his books, his garden, and his letter-writing. If his disappointments were not undeserved at least he bore them bravely; he directed and promoted his son's education till there was no more to be done, and would hardly admit defeat. When at last the young man died, and was found to have contracted a secret and undistinguished marriage—a tragi-comic climax—the old man took charge of two grandsons and wrote charming letters to their mother.

Madam,—The last time I had the pleasure of seeing you, I was so taken up in playing with the boys, that I forgot their more important affairs. How soon would you have them placed at school? When I know your pleasure as to that, I will send to Monsieur Perny, to prepare everything for their reception. In the meantime, I beg that you will equip them thoroughly with clothes, linen, &c., all good, but plain; and give me the account, which I will pay; for I do not intend that, from this time forwards, the two boys should cost you one shilling.

When Chesterfield lost his only son, and with him lost what had been his dearest interest, he had already sought consolation in a second educational venture. He made approaches to his kinsman Arthur Stanhope, whose child was his heir presumptive. When a virtual adoption was effected two series of letters began—one to the father advising on

Chesterfield

the boy's education, one to the boy himself conveying precept and example. It is natural to compare the letters to the two Philips, but they are not strictly comparable. The letters to the son extend beyond adolescence to manhood; the last to the godson was written to a boy of fifteen. Moreover, the next Earl of Chesterfield would have no bend sinister in his way, no imperative need to ingratiate himself with fortune. He had only to be good and truthful and polite and attentive (for there was a deplorable vagrancy of thought to be corrected), and the rest must follow. Lord Carnarvon ventured to discern 'a somewhat higher moral tone' in these than in the earlier letters. Mr. Dobrée, having claimed that the earlier morality is as good as the best, is reluctant to concede with any improvement; but his readers, if they reach the sixth volume, will probably agree with Carnarvon.

My dear Boy,

You are now of an age [thirteen] to be consulted, as well as taught, and therefore I desire that you will write me your sentiments upon a subject which I am not clear in myself; it is this: learning I know makes a man esteemed, virtue and honour makes him respectable, but what are in your opinion, the accomplishments that make him *aimable*? For that gives the last polish and finishing stroke to all other qualities. To a certain degree you must be aimiable, for you are beloved, and I daresay [*i.e.*, am sure] will endeavour to be more and more so every day, but what I want to know is, how you bring it about.

If the morality has not much changed it is less grimly enforced; he preaches the familiar doctrine, but with a gentler discipline.

Chesterfield

Every one thinks of Chesterfield as an old man; and perhaps the most splendid monument of his fame is Gainsborough's great portrait. 'The expression', says the *Dictionary of National Biography*, 'is cynical.' It is more than that. The hunted, searching eyes still hold us. We know very little of the young Chesterfield, *le vainqueur de la terre*, but the terrible old philosopher is still vivid. We feel that we might still quail in that presence. He grew mellower in old age. But he never hauled down his flag.

Non, Madame, le triste reste de mes jours ne vaut pas les soins que vous m'indiquez, ni l'intérêt que vous voulez bien y prendre. A soixante-huit ans, avec une constitution délabrée, et une surdité héréditaire et invétérée, j'aurais beau changer de climat, et courir le monde, on m'appliquerait avec raison
    Le chagrin monte en croupe et galoppe avec lui.
Je ne pense, et je ne dois penser, qu'à finir, tout doucement, et tuer le temps, qui est devenu mon ennemi, aussi bien que je le puis.

Lexicography[1]

THE subject of my choice has the merit of universal appeal. Everyone is interested in words, and therefore in dictionaries. Happily, however, most people are almost ignorant of lexicography. I have the less hesitation in admitting that in addressing you on this topic I shall speak as no better than an enthusiastic amateur. My practice as an empiric has, however, been varied and continuous. I crave your indulgence for a passing mention of my early struggles with the big Liddell & Scott. It was my father's copy, bound in pigskin, an incomparable, I suppose now an inaccessible, commodity for that purpose, and was nearing a century of hard wear when it lost a cover. Very greatly improved—but not out of recognition—by the labours of our time, Liddell & Scott remains one of the monuments of lexicographical expertise. I know of nothing like it in any language; and perhaps it cannot be paralleled, unless and until we have a good Latin dictionary, which the Clarendon Press is struggling to give us. The reason is this, that the limited mass of Greek literature enabled the compilers to give, for any word, not merely good illustrations of every sense, but the best illustrations. You can be sure, there, of finding all the most famous, all the most significant, and almost all the most entertaining examples. Perhaps the nearest parallel is the *Dictionary of American English*, of which Sir William Craigie is the hero. Since it confined itself to what is specifically

[1] The James Bryce Lecture delivered at Somerville College, 27 May 1948.

Lexicography

American—and stopped at 1900, before the trickle of that rip-roarious idiom became a flood—the *D.A.E.* was in a position to land all the fish and choose the best.

Emerging from the classical microcosm, I joined the staff of the Clarendon Press just after *The King's English* had burst upon the world, and Henry Watson Fowler had waked to find himself famous. I had some small share in the *Concise Oxford Dictionary*, that masterpiece of wit and miracle of comprehension. Do you know the definition of *wing*: 'One of the limbs or organs by which is effected the flight of a bird, bat, insect, angel, &c.'? Then there was the *Pocket Oxford Dictionary*, styled in its prenatal days the shilling dictionary, and designed for the great public. But the Fowlers were not really capable of stepping into that arena. They belonged to an age when levelling down was not yet esteemed a political virtue, and *P.O.D.* is in fact harder than *C.O.D.* It has, however, its own excellences; the article *numeral* was something new in lexicography, and to readers capable of interpreting it is as amusing as it is informing.

Modern English Usage was designed as a dictionary of idiom, to which in the end it did no more than approximate. We still have no such book; it is waiting for an accomplished grammarian with the nicest possible powers of discrimination.

I approached the august parent of these flippant offspring, as was but seemly, in a more cautious and gradual way. My first 'slant' upon it, my first indication that Homer could nod, I owed to my chief, Charles Cannan, a man not less witty than Fowler himself, when he remarked that the *Dictionary* 'went wrong' when Henry Bradley fell into a

Lexicography

mud hole. By this he meant that the *Dictionary* departed, at that juncture, from the scale laid down, and did so by the inclusion of too many obvious combinations and the like. The appearance of the volumes on the shelf, and the article *mud* itself, lend colour to the doctrine. But Dr. Onions disputes it, and therefore I offer it as a *bon mot* rather than as history.

My concern with the O.E.D. ceased to be merely peripheral when, many years later, I disputed with Sir William Craigie about the inordinance (as I held it) of words that begin with *un-*. His answer, though it failed to convince me, is of intrinsic interest as showing the perplexities which escape the plain man's notice and are the lexicographer's fearful joy. There are two *un*'s: when we take our ease we describe ourselves as *unbuttoned*, that is, not buttoned. But when the cannibalistic mariners invited 'little Billee' to 'unbutton the top button of your little shimmee' they were issuing a positive direction. One of my children, grasping the essence but missing the usage, used to say, 'Please button it undone.' The talk of infants throws a flood of light on phonetic change, on the formation of words,[1] and on the subtleties of idiom.

If I can claim to be in any sense a lexicographer, my apprenticeship began with the Supplement to the O.E.D. That work, the production of which took three-quarters of a century, ranged in its published form from the early eighties to the late twenties. There was therefore necessarily a large gap in modernity, and almost as inevitably a sensible gap in scale and method, between A and what

---

[1] One of my children formed 'bett'n I?' on the analogy of 'mus'n I?'.

Lexicography

I will call Z, though that letter was not in fact the last published. (You may like to know that the last word, *zyxt*, was not indeed coined, but designed for the purpose, and that our great rocket expired not with a whimper but with a comic bang.) We projected accordingly what I first called in another connexion (the *Dictionary of National Biography*) a wedge-shaped Supplement, designed to bring the work to an even date; it is, so to speak, all ABC and no XYZ. Now at this point I had some modest share in vindicating the claim to recognition of American English. Sir William Craigie, who at that time (the joke is not mine) bestrode the Atlantic 'like a colossus', was the C.-in-C., or at least the C.I.G.S., of this operation. But it was my professional duty in those years to read *The Publishers' Weekly*; and I suppose a week hardly passed that I did not cull from it one or more examples of American invention, American humour, or American ballyhoo. Many of these flowers you will find in that substantial herbarium, the Supplement of 1933.

No dictionary can do equal justice to the two great forms of the language. The result, on any grand scale, would be of superhuman bulk. The chances, moreover, are 'astronomical' against the emergence of a lexicographer, born and trained (the combination is exceedingly rare), and equally conversant with both idioms. But the belief has gained ground in this country that we ought to take notice not only of such American uses as we—of all nations the most catholic—allow to live with, often to cuckoo, our own vocables, but also of those numerous words and senses of words that reach these shores in American books, American

Lexicography

newspapers, American talk, and that range from the unintelligible to the ambiguous. Ambiguity can be dangerous; it can even create an international episode. When Dr. Abraham Flexner asked me to read the proofs of his book on Universities I was able to tell him that he must not write of 'sectional jealousies', lest he be misunderstood on this side of the Atlantic. 'Sectional' is our 'regional'; he meant not the feeling that might exist between (dare I say?) Cambridge and Swansea, which to us would mean a social antagonism, but the mutual attitude of (say) Columbia and Pasadena, 3,000 miles apart. The day I hope is past when an educated Englishman can regard 'Americanisms' as negligible dialect. If any such obscurantist survives he had better have a look at the other side of the medal, and find out what Mr. Mencken thinks of 'British English'.

The question what he shall admit, what exclude, perhaps gives the lexicographer his most *splitting* headache. A diction of an ancient language can afford to embrace everything that can be called a word. In Liddell & Scott you will find all the words known to have been written down or even, within the sacred period called classical, scratched on a wall or a potsherd. Nothing was for them too temporary (ἀρχαιομελισιδωνοφρυνιχήρατα includes *inter alia* honey, a town, and a poet) or too esoteric or too vulgar. But if the lexicographer of English should include all he finds in G. M. Hopkins and the *Daily Mirror*, that would be a phantasmagoric *olla podrida*. He must, however reluctantly, omit *drearnighted* and skies of *couple-colour*. At the other end of the scale he must draw the line, however willingly, at neologisms with which I will not sully your ears. But between

Lexicography

these extremes the choice may be very hard. Is *chalcenterous, brazen-gutted*, a dictionary word? I have not found it in any dictionary; but it is known to me and others as common 'Greats' slang; it was applied, by the late J. A. Smith, to a lexicographer who had conspicuously earned the title. The whole domain of highbrow slang, indeed, is quite a problem; it is unblushingly esoteric and polyglot—and it finds its way into *The New Statesman*. I am fond of *katakermatize*, a Platonic term for reaching the last analysis; I hope I use it with due discretion, and avoid offence to that large and worthy class that (in its heart of hearts) holds that, being ignorant of Greek, it is entitled to debar that knowledge from its peers.

It is of interest to note that American lexicographers, however conscious of their modernity, have tended to be more conservative than our own. I once asked an American to give me a definition, for some Oxford dictionary, of a word he (like everyone else I met) had just used for the tenth time. The shocked reply was, 'That isn't a dictionary word'. What, then, is a dictionary *for*? But in this exclusiveness American lexicography reflects the toryism of the American language, which has been, to our thinking, puritanically resistant to alien immigration. The explanation is, no doubt, 'defence mechanism'; a hole in the dike might have led to speedy inundation. The same motive, I take it, explains the attitude of Boston to the Irish and of New York to the Jews.

When the great dictionary that ultimately became an Oxford product was first projected, the London—or should I say London–Scottish?—dictionary, bearing the name of

Lexicography

Samuel Johnson, A.M., sometime of Pembroke College, had reigned supreme for a century. Johnson was not quite the pioneer he is sometimes thought to be. He was preceded by Bailey, who also rose to folio—though not to two folios—and was the first English lexicographer who aimed at inclusiveness, deigning even to accept *dog* and *cat*. But Bailey's was little more than an *onomasticon*, a word-book. It was Johnson who brought to English lexicography the power of discrimination and the historical sense. Sir Walter Raleigh so far forgot himself as to write that Johnson's dictionary might have been produced 'by a merely mechanical genius'. His acquaintance with the book was probably confined to its preface; but he must have known that there is no such thing as a 'mechanical genius'. The sturdy common sense that distinguishes Johnson's definitions, as it distinguishes his notes on Shakespeare, should not blind us to the delicacy of his feelings for words. He deserved to be, as he often was, quoted in the work that replaced his—*A New English Dictionary on Historical Principles*.

Everyone remembers Macaulay's snap verdict: 'Johnson was a wretched etymologist.' He does not tell us who knew any better. Who *should* etymologize, beyond the limits of the obvious, in that pre-Copernican age before philology was born? My classical-philological friends assure me that Cicero can have had no notion of the true relation of Latin and Greek. If that is so, he must have supposed *ego* and *pater* to be 'loan-words', however incredible it may seem to us that any nation should be reduced to borrowing commodities so universal. Johnson knew that the Teutonic *daughter* was the Greek θυγάτηρ; but his language on the

Lexicography

point suggests that he was as completely in the dark as Cicero.

Where Johnson was at his weakest, the *Oxford Dictionary* is at its height. The labours of many scholars of talent, and some few of genius, had brought a new technique to lexicography, and our editors helped themselves with both hands. They had, besides, other qualities. Sir James Murray added to his linguistic acumen and his tireless industry (which did not scruple to tire less chalcenterous workers) a Scotsman's hard, keen sense of the practical. Henry Bradley, who lacked that sense, had compensating virtues: he was a philologist of genius, and his sense of idiom was unsurpassable. Of their two colleagues, since they survive, I may content myself with remarking that Sir William Craigie is, like Murray, a Scot, and that Dr. Onions is, like Bradley, an Englishman. Neither is a Londoner; and that perhaps is why the dictionary does not go to extremes in recognition of the worst phonetic excesses of what is called Standard English.

And what of the future? More than sixteen years have now passed since the last word of the last volume of the *Oxford Dictionary* was written. Every day, in this age of scientific and mechanical progress, new gadgets are born and christened; every day nature is made to disclose fresh secrets, and the Greek and Latin lexicons are ransacked for appropriate coinages—the atom bomb, the electronic brain. The spirit of adventure and invention, which is active in the Anglo-American world, and is too often artificially stimulated by the perverse ingenuity of journalists, every day evolves new words or gives new twists to old ones.

Lexicography

These growths have lately been accelerated, aggravated, in the forcing-house of war. In the tangled skein of economics—I pick a single instance—the simple antinomy of *inflation* and *deflation* is found inadequate; *reflation* and *disinflation* are coined to denote new facets of the kaleidoscope. Panting lexicography toils after these vicissitudes—perhaps in vain. Can there ever be another *Oxford Dictionary*? Will *Webster's New International*, that encyclopaedia of technology, swell till it bursts? When I last saw it, ten years ago or more, it was a volume that only a strong man could handle. There is high authority for the view that the day of the comprehensive general dictionary—be it English, or American, or Anglo-American—is over. The ineluctable curse of specialization is branded upon us. There will be, no doubt, general dictionaries, great and small, purporting to tell Everyman as much as it is good for him to know. But there will be also dictionaries of natural science (which will be called dictionaries of science); dictionaries of the several sciences and technologies; dictionaries for the student of literature; pronouncing dictionaries; dictionaries of etymology. (You will rejoice to learn that Dr. Onions has for many years been working on the *O.E.E.D.*) And so on, till the catalogue surpasses the classification of the drama that we owe to the discriminating vision of Polonius.

These dire vaticinations may well be fulfilled. But it will be tragedy for the historian—of life, or of letters, or of science—if he must look not in one book, but in one of twenty, to know who first wrote *existentialism*, who first said *spiv*; to trace the origins of *movies* and *talkies*, the birth and early death of *speakies*; the controversies that once raged

Lexicography

between *big-endians* and *little-endians*, between those who said and wrote *cĭnematograph* and those who said and wrote *kīnematograph*. I would add that if, with the ever-quickening march of mind towards that goal which the late George Gordon called the goal of universal beta-minus, the plausibilities of Mr. Shaw should win acceptance for phonetic spelling, then etymology, difficult enough in all conscience already, will be made impossible for the common man. *Cinema* with an *s* will be divorced from *kinetics*; *refer*, which will be spelled with an *i*, will be in a different part of the alphabet from *reference*. Now the theory and practice of etymology are a vital part of education. No one can read Shakespeare or Milton, within, say, 75 per cent. of full appreciation, who has not an elementary knowledge of what Johnson called the pedigree of nations. A relation of mine, sometime a Principal, deplored to a learned friend the inability of her undergraduate students to spell *seize* and *siege*. The great scholar looked puzzled. 'But they must know that *seize* is *saisir*; they must know that *siege* is *siéger*.' 'Well,' was the reply, 'in fact, you know, they don't.' It has been pointed out that spelling is not only a clue to origin; it is often the cause of etymology; you could not form *bauxite* on *Les Baux* (*bo*).

I confess myself a traditionalist: not a diehard; but a believer in the Ovidian maxim *Principiis obsta*; in the Victorian doctrine of the brake on the coach; in that supreme triumph of British anomaly, the unreformed House of Lords. I regard the danger of phonetic spelling, which would convert the history of European civilization into something very like a cryptogram (putting the Bodleian out of action,

Lexicography

most of it *ubique et omnibus*, to Everyman for ever), as a real and very grave danger. Don't tell me that 'it cănt happen here'; anything can happen anywhere. If ever, on either side of the Atlantic, we enjoy the blessings of a social revolution, some zealous Shavian civil servant may easily effect, overnight, by a stroke of his pen, this 'minor and long-overdue reform'.

My mention of the alphabet reminds me of the grievance that I have long cherished against that blindest of guides. A vocabulary (unlike, in my view, an index) is necessarily alphabetical. But I have toyed with the notion of portmanteaux. Is it worth considering whether all the words that come from the Latin *cedo* (now *kaydo*, formerly *seedo*) might, while retaining their several places, be referred to a central article on *cede*? That article would tell us, once for all, that though *cedo* means *cede*, in composition it means *go*, which explains *proceed* and the rest; that its participle is *cessus* (for *cēdtus*), which explains the relation of *procession* to *proceed*; we should learn the reason (if there is one) why the *e*'s of *proceed* and *precede* are differently disposed, and why there is an *s* in *abscess*. If you will contemplate the application of this principle to all the words that mean, or once meant, *sit* (e.g. *session*, and *sederunt*, and *president*), or to all the words that derive from *scindo*, 'I cleave' (as *rescission*—but not *scissors*, which is misspelled by false etymology), or from *caedo*, 'I cut' (as *concise*, *homicide*, and *caesura*), you may agree with me that much space would be saved in etymological and other explanation, and that our dictionaries would be even more edifying, even more entertaining, than they already are.

Lexicography

The objection to the omnibus article is obvious. We all resent cross-references, especially in a work of more than one volume. But the Oxford dictionaries are already, of necessity, full of those capital letters which tell us to look elsewhere for an etymology, or a synonym, or for further information. I am sure that concentration of the words relating to many specialisms would richly repay the trouble of cross-reference by a great gain both of space and of clarity and edification. The terms of prosody, to take a good example, are very often Greek; they do not declare their meanings to all comers, and dictionaries are apt to define *obscurum per obscurius, ignotum per ignotius*. Thus the *Shorter Oxford* defines *galliambic* as 'ionic a minore tetrameter catalectic, with anaclasis', a definition compelling the ignorant to look up three, perhaps four, other words. The omnibus of my plan would collect all these terms in, perhaps, three alphabetical series: *amphibrach, anapaest, antispast* in one; *alcaic, anacreontic, asclepiad* in a second; miscellaneous terms like *catalectic, brachycatalectic, enjambement*, and *ottava rima* in a third. Using the conventional symbols for long and short, it would reduce all the feet and combinations of feet to compendious and intelligible formulae. Such an article would permit itself to be read; it would convey information which anyone consulting a single article in existing dictionaries would be likely to want, and which he would almost certainly fail to find.

The higher lexicography in this country has for long eschewed pictorial, and even diagrammatic, illustration. No one wants pretty pictures in a serious dictionary; I am not pleading for birds and butterflies, or even for the flags

Lexicography

of the nations. But we lose a lot by denying ourselves the modern counterparts of those superb copperplates which, in such a work as the *Cyclopaedia* (1728) of Ephraim Chambers, set forth the details of human anatomy or the masts and rigging of a ship. In our own age, as the *Illustrated London News* once a week reminds us, the complexities of a motor engine, a submarine, or an aeroplane can hardly be made intelligible except by pictures. A great many simpler objects—a chevron, or a cross-crosslet, or a quincunx, or a dodecahedron—are more briefly and more lucidly defined by diagram than by any form of words. Is it outside the province of lexicography to tell us how long an inch and a centimetre are? I suggest that the mystery of the subtending side, which I suppose schoolchildren are still taught to call *hypotenuse*, is best dissipated by a diagram showing to the eye that the square on the long side of a right-angled triangle is in fact equal to the sum of the other two squares: that, in other words, 16 and 9 make 25. Why should not a dictionary, itself *in pari materia*, show us by ocular demonstration the varieties of our alphabet—roman uncial, Carolingian minuscule, court hand, black-letter lower case, pica, and nonpareil?

I am not even sure that a combination of these two methods—an illustrated omnibus—might not profitably be applied to the terms of architecture; *architrave, cornice, metope, triglyph,* or *pier, pillar, pilaster, column, shaft* are most readily explained in combination. *Nail-head, dog-tooth,* and *ball-flower* take a good deal of verbal definition, but are easily and convincingly depicted. Care and skill would be needed in bringing so rich a vocabulary into one article; ease of

Lexicography

reference is essential, and a dictionary is not an encyclopaedia. But I think this problem could be solved. If, for example, the mouldings—*fillet* and *reed* and *cyma recta*, and so forth—were arranged alphabetically in one section, then the article on *fillet* would refer us, for the architectural sense, to *Architecture*, § 7, where we should find it in its place with a further reference to a number in the plate. A clear case for combining the principles of diagram and omnibus is afforded, I think, by certain trigonometrical ratios. The *Concise Oxford* defines the *sine* of an angle as 'ratio of the perpendicular subtending the angle A to the hypotenuse'. That is cumbrous, even if the reader knows the two technical terms in the definition. *Cosine* is defined as 'sine of complement of given angle', *secant* as 'ratio of greater to less of its [i.e. angle's] containing lines as bounded by a perpendicular to either', *cosecant* as 'secant of complement of given angle', *tangent* as 'ratio of the perpendicular subtending it in any right-angled triangle to the base', *cotangent* as 'tangent of complement of given angle'. Clearly, these definitions were not framed by one mind at one time, nor any one of them with regard to all the others. I submit that space would be saved and clarity gained by grouping the six terms in a single article (to which each word in its place would be referred) thus:

$$\sin a = \frac{y}{r} \qquad \cos a = \frac{x}{r}$$

$$\sec a = \frac{r}{x} \qquad \mathrm{cosec}\, a = \frac{r}{y}$$

$$\tan a = \frac{y}{x} \qquad \cot a = \frac{x}{y}$$

Lexicography

There is another way in which I believe that we might save some of the space we shall so sorely need, if we are to catch the winged words as they come from the lips of the neoterizers. I suggest, with all respect, that lexicographers deserve the description given, by a recent commission, to civil servants: they dare not take risks. Most of them (I except, of course, the Oxonians) rely mainly on the files, and one dictionary is very like another. In one particular they are always behind the times, partly because they repeat, from a predecessor, words or senses that have become obsolete, partly because (in the U.S.A. especially) native conservatism scruples to admit the eccentric, or the vulgar, or the possibly ephemeral. The *Oxford Dictionary* itself, with its eyes open (I know by whom), rejected *radium* and *vitamin*; doubtful, perhaps, how to pronounce the latter; 'vītamins', Punch had asked, 'or vĭtamines?'

The question of obsolescence demands a digression. Who shall say what is obsolete? 'Unhouseled, disappointed, unaneled': all these are in a sense as dead as Queen Anne; as dead as Shakespeare. But Shakespeare, being dead, yet speaketh; every word in *Hamlet* is part, not indeed of our common speech, but of our heritage, of our thought, of our *oral* quotation. The same is true of other perennial sources of English undefiled. There is another class of the obsolete, that which is really (whether it deserved it or not) dead and buried. But it is often difficult to decide whether a word or sense is quite dead, or moribund, or merely feeling its years; that is especially so when we deal with senses and idioms. For almost all uses of *throw*, verb transitive, *fling* is a synonym with the added notion of violence, haste,

Lexicography

temper, or the like. We can throw, or fling, something to the winds. Othello might well have called himself

> One whose hand
> Like the base Indian *flung* a pearl away.

But do we still fling dice? I cannot be sure. We have, of course, *O.E.D.* But even if the latest quotation for any word was up to the minute at the date of compilation, and it is very long odds against that, it is now twenty years old for Z and sixty for A. The lexicographer must, therefore, use his judgement, and he is too often unwilling to do so.

The conservatism of lexicography meets with a docile, even a servile, acquiescence. It was once my duty to frame a case against a manifest thief: a lexicographer who had copied the *C.O.D.*, on the whole very skilfully, but ever and again nodding, like Homer, and so producing tell-tale nonsense by missing the point of one of Fowler's subtle devices. But when I submitted my findings to an eminent King's Counsel his reply was, in effect: 'Of course you are right; rank plagiarism. But you will find no jury, and precious few judges, who can be made to see it. You will only burn your fingers.'

I return to my projected economy. One of the things the 'harmless drudge' finds it easiest to do, and so perhaps is glad to do for relaxation, is to note the derivatives formed by suffixes. Now almost every noun, unless euphony forbids, can make an adjective by adding *-less*: *useless*, *needless*, *heedless*, *meatless*, and if you like—why not?—*matchless*, *tobaccoless*, *potatoless*. Some of these are, we hope, ephemeral. In any case they, and a thousand like them, are made at will, and may be assumed. Any adjective, subject to the

Lexicography

phonetic limitation, can make a noun in *-ness*: *fidgetiness, pernickitiness, blindness, obtuseness, one-track-mindedness*; the catalogue of sins that lexicographical flesh is heir to might be extended indefinitely. I submit that a sentence in a preface, or a footnote to a list of live suffixes, would be a sufficient direction.

Lexicographical treatment of proper names has varied. Lewis & Short is full of them, Liddell & Scott has none. The *O.E.D.* set out with a principle of rigid exclusion; so much so as to exclude *African*. It was very soon seen that the door could not be kept as tight shut as that; the principle was relaxed; *American* was let in the ground floor, *African* on the top floor, the Supplement. But once the door is ajar, the opening tends to widen. I can state a rule, but its application is hazardous. We omit, I think, Sparta, and welcome Olympia. We include Yorkshire, in virtue of its pudding, and exclude—I am afraid—Bedfordshire. I have maintained, against good authority, that whereas *Oxford shoes* must be allowed, as being shoes of a certain kind but makeable anywhere, there is no case for *Oxford marmalade*. I should admit the *Oxford accent*, on the ground that it is not exclusively Oxonian (if, indeed, it is Oxonian at all). The rule is more easily applied to names of persons. We exclude John Smith and even Shakespeare, Dogberry, and Fitzwilliam Darcy. We admit Daniel, because we can say '*A* Daniel come to judgement', and, I suppose, Hitler ('Oliver Cromwell was a Hitler'); equally, we admit Paul Pry and Simon Pure as having been generalized. Places, things, and institutions are more difficult. I notice that dictionaries admit the stars, though a star is unique, which

Lexicography

John Smith is not. But if musicians say 'What this country wants is a Bayreuth', does that amount to generalization? It is an odd thing, that, though unique institutions are nearly always excluded in their perfect form, the R.A. and the B.B.C., I believe even the L.M.S., are almost universally embraced.

The rule, however necessary, has unhappy results, and I should infringe it, if the liberty were worth getting, on almost any pretext. Sir William Craigie's article, in the *Dictionary of American English*, on *American* is a veritable epitome, in a few columns, of three centuries of American life; but there is no article on *America*, and the etymology of *American* stops short at the noun. Was not this a golden opportunity missed? I know of no book of reference that will tell me by whom, or when, or how, the word was made. Doubtless it is an adjective, *America Terra*, like *Africa*; for the basic Latin for an African is *Afer*. But why, I wonder, *América*? If, as I am assured, Vespucci was *Amerigo*, might we hope to find *Americ̆a* in some early verse?

A yawning gap in our reference shelf is a good *Dictionary of Proper Names*. The only book I know in English is the *Century Encyclopaedia*. Of that the latest edition is nearly forty years old. It includes, I think, all cities in the U.S.A. (you have guessed its origin) with over 4,000 inhabitants, and leaves out (for aught I remember) Auchinleck, Chalfont St. Giles, Ecclefechan, Steventon—perhaps even Mount Vernon. A recent American dictionary, though it boasts a gazetteer, omits Sulgrave. The *Dictionary of Proper Names* of my ambition would tell us all sorts of things for which we have now to look long, and often in vain. It would tell us—both in articles on a name, and in portmanteau-articles, and

Lexicography

by use of cross-reference—that the railway stations of London are Paddington and so on, of New York the Grand Central, the Pennsylvania Terminal, and so on; that the Bakerloo (an enigma, I find, to even well-informed young people) was once content to link Baker Street to Waterloo; that the Duke of Devonshire's name is Cavendish, and that he lives at Chatsworth, and in more ducal times lived in Devonshire House; that Marjoribanks is called Marchbanks, and that Cirencester is or was called Ciceter; that the chief cricket-grounds of England are Lords, Trent Bridge, and so on, our great golf-courses St. Andrews, Westward Ho!, and so on. It would indicate, individually and collectively, the county towns, the assize towns, the cathedral cities. It would even, if space allowed, tell us why the county of Durham is not called Durhamshire, and by what right the county whose county-town is Exeter comes to be called Devon*shire*. It might tell us that Harley St. and Wimpole St. have fallen from the pinnacle of fashion (you will recall that Mrs. Rushworth in *Mansfield Park* looked forward to opening one of the best houses in Wimpole St.) and have become the *Citadel* of a mere profession; that Grub St. is or was the slum of literature. It might even tell us that our own Beaumont St. was once Bewmónt St., and that a handful of dotards (of both sexes!) still call St. Aldate's St. Old's and St. Mary Hall Skimmery; or (if the compiler were a bigoted Oxonian) that Lord Abingdon's name is Bertie (pron. Bartie) and that a Lord Abingdon was once the owner of Wytham Abbey.

The methodology and typographical technique of lexicography have been laboriously evolved. I have wondered

Lexicography

how many readers of the Oxford dictionaries (which at one time had an incredible sale in Japan) fully apprehend, for example, the use of brackets, capitals, or italic. The etymology of *dulness* is given thus: 'dull+NESS', that is, see the suffix *-ness*. 'First class', the noun, would be defined as '(person obtaining) a place in the first division of an examination'. A sense of *fruits* might be 'reward *of* victory, &c.' This is not pedantry; the idiom might have been 'he deserved the fruits from his labours'. When the late Sir Henry Stuart Jones addressed himself to the formidable task of revising Liddell & Scott from the devoted labours of many scholars, he and I had long debates on method. It was he who invented the symbol *lyr.* that distinguished, in Greek tragedy, the choral parts, which are in a kind of Doric, from the dialogue, which is Ionic; the two dialects differ in vocabulary as well as in phonetics. It was I, I think, who suggested the use of italic for names of books, which enabled us to reduce the *Agamemnon* of Aeschylus from 'Aesch. Ag.' to 'A.*Ag.*'. We tried to adopt the well-established convention which calls the first Iliad A and the last Odyssey ω; but we were beaten by the ambiguity of A. A1 would have meant μῆνιν ἄειδε. But it might have meant the first section of Class A. There are, unhappily, no Greek capitals for those letters which the Greek alphabet has in common with the Roman.[1]

There is always room at the top. In the yet-unfinished

---

[1] Another lexicographer's bogy is consistency. If we had been prepared to make exceptions, and print *Il.* A 1 or *Od.* B 2, to avoid ambiguity, we could have abridged the great majority of the references to such unambiguous compendia as Δ 477 or ϕ 201. 'Thank God we needn't be consistent' was a remark of Fowler.

Lexicography

Oxford dictionary, the '*Unconcise* Dictionary of Modern English', there will be a startling innovation, the nature of which I must not reveal.

English lexicography, when conducted on the grand scale, is not a little embarrassed by the lack of adequate references to our prose literature. Even our verse-references might be better. *Hamlet*, IV. iii. 77 is a cumbrous notation; and whereas every scholar can discover in a moment, if he does not remember it, how much longer the *Oedipus at Colonus* is than the *Prometheus Vinctus*, it takes a painful calculation to determine the precise quantitative relation between *Hamlet* and *Macbeth*: a matter, of course, of moment, since *Hamlet* may not be unitary, and *Macbeth* may have been cut. Again, while Aeschylus' play is always *P.V.*, it is not yet settled (in spite of Dr. Onions's labours) whether *Romeo and Juliet* is *Rom.* or *R.J.* There is no recognized abbreviation for *The Ring and the Book*; if it were a work of classical antiquity it would probably be known as R.B., R.B. When we come to prose, confusion is worse confounded. The reference 365A or 1365b finds the place in every text or translation of Plato or Aristotle in every part of the globe. The convention is oecumenical. But you cannot refer to all editions of the *Life of Johnson* except by the date, a clue which will not lead to every passage in even that scrupulously chronological work, or to all editions of *Tom Jones* except by the chapter-numbers. It is time, I suggest, for the British Academy to charge an academician, or a committee of wranglers, to devise a notation for our prose classics. But perhaps I shall deserve my answer: 'I wonder that you will still be talking, Signior Benedick; nobody marks you.'

S.P.E.: Retrospect[1]

WHEN I addressed myself to the honourable, melancholy task of writing the obsequy of S.P.E., I revived fond memories by turning over my file. I found there the original prospectus and first list of (fourteen) members, bearing the date 1913. This was 'for private circulation only'. It was not until 1919 that the Society issued Tract No. I, which added to a reprint of the original prospectus a further statement of its principles and aims, with a longer list of members. Today our founder, Robert Bridges, O.M., Poet Laureate, and most of his active colleagues—whether as framers of policy or as authors of the tracts—have according to their several skills or predilections pronounced their last judgement, flown their last linguistic kite, pointed their last epigram, or split their last infinitive.[2] We have lost Lascelles Abercrombie, Henry Bradley, Henry Watson Fowler, George Gordon, Walter Raleigh,[3] John Sargeaunt, Logan Pearsall Smith. The handful of surviving torch-bearers have found it necessary to close a chapter, which all lovers of good English must hope will be followed by a longer series. It can hardly be hoped that the cause will ever be in wiser hands.

---

[1] Society for Pure English, Tract the Sixty-Sixth and Last, 1948.
[2] See Tract XV.
[3] Raleigh was (as he quoted of himself in another connexion) rather a buttress than a column of the Society. But the name, as cofounder, of so unprofessional a professor made it clear that the Society's interest was not less literary than it was philological.

S.P.E.: Retrospect

The history of the Society exhibits in the founder a shrewd business sense that surprised any who had seen in the sage of Chilswell only a poet-philosopher of ample means and leisure. It began its career with studied modesty: a handful of members, and no subscription. The early tracts were printed and published by the Clarendon Press (to which the nod of Bridges was as good as an order of the Delegates) without contract or even verbal agreement. But the infant society quickly put on dignity and solvency. There were at first no minutes. But at a meeting held at Corpus Christi College in December 1925 it was unanimously agreed that

Whereas it has hitherto been our custom to make no record of our conferences, the prosperity of the Society now demands that a written record of the meetings should be kept, which in case of enquiry would testify to the unanimity of the Committee and to their individual responsibility in the disposition of the accumulated funds, there being at the present date a balance at the Bank of £263. 9 11, and a credit at the Clarendon Press of £254. 8.

Meetings of the committee were convivial and not very numerous. But the minutes furnish copious evidence of the Society's way of work, of the high standard expected of its contributors (who were moreover paid on a generous scale), and of the influence exerted by the Society on the English-speaking world. The Society had a secretary, whose office was no sinecure. But she did not keep the minutes, which are in the well-known hand of the founder[1] and bear every

---

[1] They were continued after his death in the equally beautiful, more regularly calligraphic, hand of his widow.

S.P.E.: Retrospect

mark of his style. They were signed by all the members present. It will surprise no one to learn that all resolutions were unanimous. If dictatorship by consent be the truest democracy, the S.P.E. was indeed democratic.

Occasional touches of *hauteur* will not be denied a mention. Once it was 'voted that no audit is needed'. Several times a letter is 'read and put aside'. References to 'the British Broadcasting Association' and later to the B.B.C. are respectful but critical. It may be recalled that S.P.E. did not always approve the pronunciations 'vulgarized' by the B.B.C.

As the Society advanced in prosperity and reputation, the metropolitan committee-men, whose activities are so largely devoted to organizing our language and its literature, sensed that here was a good thing. It is known—of course off the record—that on one occasion at least they made the descent from London, expecting to pounce on an unresisting quarry. They found they had started a tiger. When a Society, long established and resonantly named, was suggested as offering its aegis to the infant growth, Bridges growled that he hadn't heard of it; 'Is it any good?' The sportsmen returned with an empty bag.

The quality of the Society's tracts is always good, often very good. Bridges himself was no more than an amateur as philologist, phonetician, and orthoepist. But he was a linguist; he had long pondered his own language, and had an intimacy of knowledge that came from laborious, fastidious, and accomplished handling of it in verse and prose. Nor was his learning tainted with preciosity; his own speech was homespun. He was saved from extravagance in the pursuit of 'pure' English by his native good sense, and from

S.P.E.: Retrospect

serious error by the counsel of Henry Bradley. The friendship and collaboration of the two men can be read in their published correspondence, or inferred from the Society's tracts. The quality of their unrecorded exchanges may be easily guessed from the letters, in which ever and again Bridges advances a paradox, somewhat irresponsibly or provocatively, and Bradley replies with a cautious concatenation of provisos and discriminations. He did not split hairs; but he could see real distinctions where the plain man saw an atom.

Bradley's direct contribution was lamentably slender. The claims of the *Oxford Dictionary* on his failing health were paramount. Bridges, not quite unreasonably, regarded this work as wasteful of his friend's transcendent gifts, and never scrupled to interrupt him at his desk in the Old Ashmolean and pick his brains or draw his fire on some point of metre or pronunciation. The quality of Bradley's secondary contribution is nowhere better seen than in the preface and footnotes by which, in Tract IV, he neutralized the effect of certain *mumpsimuses* to which Sargeaunt, sinning against the light, obstinately adhered. He had promised a discussion on *Briton, Britisher*, and kindred words: a subject more apt to generate heat than light. Death put an end to preoccupation and hesitancy, and Bridges was able to publish only a page of preamble.

As Bridges's influence pervaded and dominated his society, so his multifarious interests initiated, dictated, or coloured its work. He was in general the Society's chief exponent, apologist, and advertising manager. He expatiated, in particular, he let himself go, on the darling topics of phonetics

S.P.E.: Retrospect

(and especially of homophones, the baleful influence of which he doubtless over-stated), of spelling reform (but this *pedetemptim*), of the functions of poetry in education, of the use of dialect in literature. Prosody is surprisingly lacking; but he was frying that fish in another pan. When he needed help, he knew where to find it. Experts swam eagerly into his orbit to pronounce on the language of anatomy (9, Dr. W. C. Morton) and physics (48, Sir Charles Darwin), or to illuminate, historically and aesthetically, the mysteries of handwriting (23 and 28, Dr. E. A. Lowe, Roger Fry, and Mr. Alfred Fairbank).[1] The relation of English to other languages, and to abstract Language, was not overlooked. Mr. Paul Barbier (7) discussed the influence of English on the French vocabulary; Matthew Barnes,[2] inquiring (8) 'What is Pure French?', generalized the vexing problem of purity; and the late Brander Matthews (5) exposed the pitfalls that beset us when we seek to naturalize French words. Mr. Charles T. Carr (42) discussed German influences on English. Sir Richard Paget (22) was given a forum for his bold speculations on 'The Nature of Human Speech'; and the redoubtable Professor Jespersen of Copenhagen (16) was allowed (in anticipation of the later evolution of philosophy?) to explore the shifting frontier where Grammar marches with Logic. Mr. R. C. Goffin (44) contributed from experience an essay on Indian English. Re-

---

[1] These two tracts, which are an important addition to the literature on handwriting, are fully illustrated—from Raphael and Bembo to Ludwig Traube and Mr. Stanley Morison. The plates show good writing in varying conditions, including a letter from a lady of eighty, and the last entry in the diary of Captain Scott. The introductions are by Bridges.

[2] I rejoice to learn that this was a pseudonym for Monica Bridges, R.B.'s wife.

S.P.E.: Retrospect

turning to base, the late Henry Cecil Wyld (39) put up a stout defence of 'standard' English (which he spoke to admiration) as the best, Mr. Eric Partridge (55) outgrossed Gross in a spate of slang, and only the other day Mr. G. M. Young (62) was called in to undermine the foundations of 'Basic English'.

The chief concern of the Society overseas was of course with American English. Perhaps Bridges's only disappointment was the meagre response to his appeal for contributions from the United States. Professor Fred Newton Scott (24) did compile a short list of slang terms 'for British readers struggling with the works of Sinclair Lewis'. For the rest the task was left entirely to British 'transients', and almost entirely to one man. Mr. H. W. Horwill, the author of *Modern American Usage*, wrote an important essay (24) on 'American Variations': the difference given, by the American way of life, to common words like *elector* or *public school* or *lovely* or *homely*—a difference often productive of embarrassing or even perilous misconceptions. But the other tracts that deal with American English—and their bulk is substantial—were by Sir William Craigie, who by his dictionary work on British, Scottish, and American English, and by his long residence in Chicago, was perhaps uniquely equipped. Persons almost equally conversant with the two main dialects of English are common enough; trained lexicographers are rare; the combination is very rare. Restored to Oxfordshire, and endowed at last with the nearest approach he has known to leisure, Sir William has had a copious late flowering. His contributions began in 1927 with 'The Study of American English' (27). In the

S.P.E.: Retrospect

war-years he has carried the torch of S.P.E. almost alone. His American contribution in this period is a substantial 'double' (56 and 57) on 'The Growth of American English'.

Dr. C. T. Onions, the youngest of the four Atlantes who shouldered the vast bulk of the *Oxford Dictionary*, τετράγωνον ἄνευ ψόγου τετυγμένον, resembles his master Bradley in sticking closely to his last. Only one tract bears his sole name: 61, on French *-é* in English and on plurals in *-ths*. He is also the author of two notes, on *broadcast* v. *broadcasted* (in 19), and on *distance no object* (in 36).

Mr. Kenneth Sisam, who also worked at one time in the Old Ashmolean, was throughout active in the Society's deliberations, and its minutes suggest that he did a good deal of anonymous editorial work. Preoccupation combined with his native economy to deny him the authorship of any whole tract. His dozen pages on 'Word-division' (in 33) exhibit those qualities of lucidity and comprehension that his admirers look for, and sometimes find, in learned journals.

Lascelles Abercrombie came late to Oxford and the S.P.E. committee, and he, too, made only a slight contribution, 'Colloquial Language in Literature' (in 36). It is interesting to note a community of taste with his brother poet. Bridges had explored the use of dialect in Mr. Blunden's poetry; Abercrombie confessed that he preferred Mr. P. G. Wodehouse's to James Joyce's 'experiments in writing'.

George Gordon, an early though not an original member of the committee, was alone among his colleagues in his strictly historical approach to the matters that concerned the Society. His tracts are 'Medium Aevum' (19) and 'Shakespeare's English' (29). He was by profession a Shakespearian,

S.P.E.: Retrospect

by temperament a student of the tools of literature; Shakespeare's verbal wizardry was a topic to which he often recurred. Insatiable curiosity had made him, as he would say, a dabbler in medieval studies. 'Medium Aevum' is perhaps his only public sortie into that distant region. Both tracts have the marks of his acute and generous intelligence.

Two non-resident Oxonians were especially active: Logan Pearsall Smith and Henry Watson Fowler. Pearsall Smith, who had often lived in or near Oxford, and was always a frequent visitor, was one of Bridges's elder disciples, and in this enterprise for long his right-hand man. He was widely known as an entertaining writer and a romantic—perhaps over-romantic—amateur of English words in all their facets. The Society gave him opportunities, of verbal speculation and of piety, which he did not miss. He wrote tracts on 'English Idiom' (12), on 'Romantic, Originality, Creative, Genius' (17), and finally 'Fine Writing' (46). The *Oxford Dictionary* was never far from his elbow in his bookroom in Chelsea, and he was tireless in tracing origins and following developments. If these gave a target for whimsical cynicism, so much the better. At an early stage he had offered (in 3) 'A Few Practical Suggestions'; and after Bridges's death he wrote 'Recollections' of the founder in Tract 45, to which Bridges's daughter, Mrs. Daryush, contributed 'His Work on the English Language'. Smith had lived much with men of genius or talent. He had an almost Boswellian memory, and a passion for biography; the *Dictionary of National Biography* was a favourite book. His rippling malice concealed, moreover, a faculty of veneration which such a subject did not fail to put in motion. The tract

S.P.E.: Retrospect

includes a moving paragraph on Mrs. Bridges's skill and devoted help.

Henry Watson Fowler shared with Bridges the honour of an obituary by the S.P.E. This (43) was written by George Gordon Coulton, who had known him at Sedbergh and had kept up with him. The record was mainly personal. It told many, who knew only the versatile lexicographer, that Fowler was a man with a steely conscience and a soft heart. He never, on principle, entered the church which he saw from the window of his home in Somerset. But his wife was a devout church-goer. When she died, he had the bells re-hung, that they might 'ring again as she heard them'. Very unlike the other chief contributors, Fowler was a recluse. He had not seen Oxford since he took his degree, and nothing would persuade him to break the spell. He was, however, known to many of us by correspondence, as to countless thousands by his works. The S.P.E. gave him a chance of exercising and sharpening his rapier on monsters he had scotched but not killed, or of returning to the rescue of injured innocence. He was the sole author of Tract 6, on 'Hyphens, *shall* and *will*, &c.', and of 10, 'On Grammatical Inversion'. He contributed, to other tracts, articles on metaphor (11), on the split infinitive (15; he was a stout defender of this fissure, when properly made), and on the 'fused' participle (22).

The writer of this survey was not of the elect. But he was graciously permitted, on one occasion invited, to ventilate his notions in these tracts. To one of them, 'Oxford English' (37), he was stung, when on a visit to the United States, by certain intemperate denunciations, by American

S.P.E.: Retrospect

patriots, of what is called standard English. In 'Names, Designations, and Appellations' (47) he ventured beyond the frontiers of lexicography to investigate the idiom of polite British English in such nuances as distinguish the use of 'Mrs. Jones', 'my wife', and 'Mary' respectively. In 'Adjectives from Proper Names' (52) he explored *inter alia* the implications of the history of the English pronunciation of Latin, which had been lucidly set forth by Sargeaunt in Tract 4.

An outsider, then, comparatively speaking, may be allowed to claim for this Society that it did in its generation a signal service to the language which so many love and so few know how to use. A handful of busy academics, few of them able to command much leisure or to boast any notoriety, led by a poet-philosopher who was known to the millions as the silent laureate, they went their own informal way, knowing no party and grinding no axe. Yet they achieved, by mere knowledge, judgement, and integrity, a position of outstanding authority. The tracts are still too little known; but their power has flowed, and flows, in many channels, and they will not be quickly forgotten.

Other Reviews

Poetic Diction[1]

MR. QUAYLE proposes a study 'both literary and linguistic'; he will discuss 'literary conditions', but he will also 'deal with the words themselves'. This raises our hopes; for generalizations are of little value in such a case, and we have had too many. But we are doubtful if Mr. Quayle has pursued the inductive method with sufficient rigour.

Since the whole subject cannot be briefly discussed without obscurity, we confine ourselves to Mr. Quayle's treatment of Latinism—an amusing and not unimportant topic. A Latinism, we suppose, is a word of Latin origin which (*a*) is so unfamiliar as to remain un-English, or (*b*) is used in a sense which is un-English. Mr. Quayle, who applies the term to many words which are common in eighteenth-century poetry, does not offer a definition of it; and he seems uneasily conscious that he is not ready with a definition. He would like to think of his Latinisms as coinages; Gray, he tells us, abstained 'from any indulgence in coinages'. But he knows, of course, that Thomson and Cowper did not in fact invent the words of which they have been supposed the authors. So he takes refuge in the theory that 'their "poetic" use is first due to' these writers. 'Cowper's latinized words appear to have been floating about for a considerable period, though in most cases their first poetic use is apparently due to him.' But this argument from the silences of the *Oxford Dictionary* proves nothing; if a word

---

[1] *T.L.S.* 25 Dec. 1924: Review of Thomas Quayle, *Poetic Diction*.

Poetic Diction

is 'floating about', surely a poet may pick it up. Finally, Mr. Quayle knocks down his house of cards by the suggestion that Gray's occasional Latinisms 'were still current in the language of the time'.

He feels himself on surer ground when he finds an English word used in a Latin sense, and makes the most, accordingly, of the examples he can muster. But here his study of the history has been perfunctory. He several times cites 'prevent', used as in 'Prevent us O Lord'. But though Johnson says that 'hinder' is 'now almost the only sense' of that word, it is clear that the other sense was quite familiar, though it may have passed out of colloquial use. Was there anything artificial in Thomson's use of 'horrid'? 'The Apennines', wrote Gray from Italy, 'are not so horrid as the Alps.' 'Secure', in its original sense, was good ordinary English in Jane Austen's time. Goldsmith's 'vacant mind' is misunderstood by modern schoolboys, but was perhaps unambiguous to his contemporaries. Johnson has 'vacant to futurity', and he quotes this from Wotton: 'The Duke of Buckingham had a pleasant and vacant face, proceeding from a singular assurance in his temper.'

It might be possible to force Mr. Quayle into a definition of what is not a Latinism, from his statement that Goldsmith uses only three. These are (1) 'vacant mind', (2) 'gelid wings', (3) 'indurated heart'. The evidence suggests that 'indurated' was a less uncommon word than it is now. If 'gelid wings' is a Latinism, wherein does it differ from 'tepid wave'? The answer may be that 'tepid' was in colloquial use and that 'gelid' was not; but Mr. Quayle is not in a position to assert this; all we learn from him is that

Poetic Diction

'gelid' was very common in 'neo-classical' verse, and that he dislikes it. He is, indeed, conscious of the need to discriminate between those Latin words which, 'in virtue of their long employment', have 'acquired that force and picturesqueness which the poet needs', and 'the Latinized words of the eighteenth century'. But when he attempts to state the difference his objectivity forsakes him, and he is content to protest that 'To us, nowadays, there is something pretentious and pedantic about them'. Quite so. But we want to know why, and Mr. Quayle has not told us. He does not tell us what is wrong with 'gelid'; he does not tell us wherein the vice, whatever it is, is peculiar to his period, or why Thomson's gelid this and gelid that are more offensive than Ben Jonson's gelid sighs or Marvell's gelid strawberries. Finally, he does not tell us what was wrong in the attitude of the poets themselves to their vocabulary. He complains that they were not 'able to give a poetical colouring to such words'; and that they were led by a literary fashion 'to seek in mere words qualities which are to be found in them only when they are the reflex of profound thought or powerful emotion'. But this, surely, is to confuse bad tools with a bad use of tools. In all ages bad poets, or poets writing badly, use the poetic vocabulary at second hand, to express emotions which they do not feel. That a poem, or a pudding, is heavy and insipid, tells us nothing about the ingredients employed.

We do not suggest that there is in fact no such thing as eighteenth-century Latinism. But we are afraid the material still awaits analysis.

Sir Walter Raleigh's Letters[1]

SIR WALTER RALEIGH left behind him a large number of essays in criticism, which are highly esteemed by students of literature, and a few pamphlets on the war, or on topics arising out of the war, which are as yet little known. He left also the memory, vivid but incommunicable, of wonderful talk—talk as wise as it was playful, as sane as it was brilliant. His friends have preserved many of his familiar letters, which are very like his talk; and from these his widow has printed a selection. It was all that could be done, and all that was necessary. There is no need to write his life. These letters, with Mr. Nichol Smith's brief introduction, supply all the commentary on his works that posterity will require. If future generations neglect his works, they will require nothing that we can give them.

Raleigh was a scholar. He succeeded, by his incautious talk, in persuading many of his Oxford acquaintances (who were willing enough to be so persuaded) that he was no scholar. That this view was mistaken his friends knew; and it can be proved from his letters. They show, for instance, that he knew all about the question, which though vexed is little understood, of English spelling. His dicta on this subject, if put together, will be found to cover the ground. In the first place, phonetic spelling is an absurdity, because it assumes a uniformity which does not exist and must not be created. 'You must teach people a pronunciation harder and clearer than is needed for daily speech. Then let them

[1] *T.L.S.* 11 Feb. 1926: Review of the selection by Lady Raleigh.

Raleigh's Letters

soften the edges to taste.' 'There is a kind of Platonic ideal underlying all daily usage. It is more explicit, accurate, and pedantic than anyone's daily speech.' Again, phonetic spelling, or any spelling which it may be sought to impose by the authority of experts, is an unwarrantable infringement of liberty. 'This language, these words, belong to everyone. You can't change spelling usage, or table manners, or family names, by authority. You've got to win your public.' Raleigh's views on prohibition in another sphere were well known; and he would have liked to advocate Free Spelling. The letters show his appreciation of all sorts of aspects of spelling which have little or nothing to do with pronunciation. He inquires about the history of *He* for *he* in reference to God.

I do not find it in the 16th and 17th centuries—the age of capitals. My impression is that it is a fruit of 19th century High Church Romanticism, and was introduced by men who were capable of pronouncing even a pronoun with unction. The use of the capital, like the unctuous pronunciation, causes a quite perceptible little hitch in the flow of the thought.

There are some delightful exercises, variations on the old licence.

The cheif vertew of my reform is that it makes the spelynge express the moode of the wryter. Frinsns, if yew fealin frenly, ye kin spel frenlylike. Butte if yew wyshe to indicate that . . . yew are compleatly atte one wyth the aristokrasy you canne double alle youre consonnantts. . . .

(Charles Lamb knew that the *b* of *plumb pudding* made it 'fatter and more suetty'.)

It is important to insist that Raleigh was, in his way,

Raleigh's Letters

a man of learning. Most of his published work was in criticism, and its chance of survival might suffer if the view were current that it is insecurely based. There is no need for uneasiness. His knowledge was wide enough and deep enough to serve as matter for his perceptions and as a channel for his thought. But he was aware that detailed investigation was 'not his job'—he was meant for better things—and he did right to resist its blandishments.

> Once I thought that knowledge grew from more to more, and in thy wisdom make me wise, and all that sort of thing. But the swells didn't do the trick that way; and when I sit down to mature, I just quietly rot, or fiddle with arranging details. (1903.)

He believed in the kind of thinking which, because its processes are mysterious, we call intuitive—'we can all think justly when we are exhilarated and heated by thought'—and he knew that such thinking can only be worked out by passionate concentration. He was naturally indolent; but his best work was done in an agony. The results were sometimes surprising to himself; but he trusted them, knowing them to be his best. He writes thus of his essay on Matthew Arnold:

> I like it, but an odd thing happened to it. It came out much more hostile than I intended or than I knew I thought. That's a funny thing about writing, if you shut yourself up. You find out what you really think. Now I sat down to write an appreciation of a great critic, and found out that I didn't think so at all. (1912.)

and thus of his essay on Burns:

> I had a nine days' agony, and finished yesterday, and sent it

Raleigh's Letters

off. I think it's the best thing I've ever written, but how should I know? . . . It don't come out till October, and then in a 30/- 2 vol., handsome, illustrated reprint of Lockhart's Life. So no one will ever see it, but it's the best essay on R. B. for all that. (1914.)

It has been said in Oxford common rooms that Raleigh did not care about truth and consistency; that he was a maker of epigrams; that he was a schoolboy of genius. These judgements have a grain of truth. They were provoked by his courage and simplicity, his love of adventure, his contempt of caution. He said the first thing that came into his mind, and then looked at it to see if it would do. It might be true—and if so, he was not going to shut his eyes because it was inconsistent with something he had said ('I never remember what I say') or printed. If 'schoolboy of genius' is a criticism of Raleigh's intellectual power, or of his intellectual honesty, it is tragically false. No one who is fit to read his best essays, or the best of these letters, can fail to see that truth was his one intellectual passion. This book is full of judgements which are ill considered, or incomplete, or even wrong. But they are experimental. When Raleigh wanted to know what he really thought, he shut himself up and wrestled with the devil 'who hates to find us thinking justly'. When he emerged, he offered the result to his friends; for example, the essay on Halifax to W. P. Ker:

who I hope will like it, because it is not new-fangled or nonsensical, but just true. (1910.)

Perhaps the most important thing in these letters is that they tell us Raleigh's opinion of some of his books. They

Raleigh's Letters

authorize us, for example, to regard *Style* as partly a joke—a good joke. They tell us what he tried to do in *Milton*:

> I hope I have ended the career of the pietistic old gentleman of scholarly habits who wrote good works for Sunday afternoon reading, and have restored the blazing and acrid visionary. (1900.)

They tell us, what it is important we should know, that he believed *England and the War* to be, of all his writings, most likely to survive him. The only claim which he made publicly was in the preface:

> The only parts of this book for which I claim any measure of authority are the parts which describe the English character. No one of purely English descent has ever been known to describe the English character, or to attempt to describe it. . . . I have more Scottish and Irish blood in my veins than English; and I think I can see the English character truly, from a little distance.

But in the letters we learn more than this:

> My book, though I say it, is a daisy. Hardly any of it is wrong. I was surprised to find how well it wears against the facts.
>
> The little book will some day be a famous book. I told Lucie this; I never said it, or thought it, of any other of my books. (1918.)

These passages, and many more, show that, if Raleigh is to be taken seriously, his published works are his monument. But the letters will be more popular today; and of that no one need complain. If they are less deep than his essays, they are wider. They recall the summer lightning of his talk, which played on the surface of a subject, and often

Raleigh's Letters

flashed to its heart. They have all the qualities which give joy to colloquial speculation. They are irresponsible and irrelevant, like a child; and, like a child, they may at any moment, without regard to consequences or decorum, blurt out a truth.

Much that is in these volumes Raleigh could not have printed. We commend the courage that has given us his unexpurgated opinions. We have the truth as he saw it on many still burning questions—on Thackeray and Meredith, on Froude and Arnold, on Stevenson and Henley, on Gladstone and Chamberlain, on Mr. Bradley and Mr. Bridges.

Thackeray is only a Plymouth brother caught tuft hunting and pretending that he was in fun. (1901.)

He's a dreadful man, superior to the last gasp, and incurably sentimental in what I call a timid way. Also damd moral. He's no use at all to me. But of course those who really like him are right, as all those who really like anything are right, and I never interfere or decry. (1918.)

Raleigh's estimate of the importance of literary criticism was never high; and as he grew older he grew more impatient of his trade. He wrote to a fellow augur:

God forgive us all! If I am accused on Judgment Day of teaching literature, I shall plead that I never believed in it and that I maintained a wife and children. (1921.)

He tired not only of writing and teaching, but even of reading, which had ceased to stimulate his thought. The war furnished fresh problems, and during those four years he thought, on occasion, as hard as ever. *England and the War* shows that inaction and suspense could not dull his mind or sour his thinking. But he grew visibly fatigued. The invitation to be the historian of the War in the Air, with all it meant of experience and adventure, made a boy of him once more. His enthusiasm, his avidity of information were inexhaustible. It is impossible, now, to regret that he suffered absurd unnecessary hardships in the desert, and came home from Baghdad to correct his last proofs, and to die.

He has been heard to say that he ought, in his youth, to have passed through the mill of literary journalism; and once in these letters (but once only?) he says that he 'ought to have written about things'. But we doubt if he died leaving much unwritten that it was in him to write. He used to say that the best things in the *Lives of the Poets* are the incidental comments on life. This is true of his own critical essays; and his range of subjects was wider than Johnson's. Remembering his Burns, his Blake, his Voyagers, his Age of Elizabeth, his Don Quixote, we need not suppose his genius to have been trammelled by the topics to which circumstances directed it. He knew that his glimpses of truth were partial. That was one reason why he did not worry about consistency, or recognize any obligation to form his mind on all questions of moment. When, in 1918, he was offered a seat in Parliament, he had to reply that

oddly enough, I don't know which is my party. My friends, many of them, tell me I am a Liberal; and so far as the Whig party embodies the national tradition, I suppose I am a Whig.

It is permissible to doubt his Liberalism. But there is no doubt of his Democracy. Yachting with Sir Hubert Parry, he studied the Irish character.

Sir H. Parry was very funny; he on board (with a cook), they

Raleigh's Letters

on shore (with farms). He is a sound Radical, self-indulgent, but touched by a sense of guilt towards others less fortunate. They will be all right, he says, when they manage their own affairs, and quite prosperous. But the devil of it is there are things they like better than prosperity.

I am awfully comfortable among them. Ireland is a perfect nest for all that is most profoundly unsatisfactory in my temper and character. So I love the Irish; and Sir H. Parry dislikes them quite acutely. I remember that Adamson, who was a Radical, hated men in public-houses (whom I often like). There must be some cause for all this. (1912.)

It is natural to write of these letters mainly as they exhibit the intellectual explorer. But intellectual adventure is not the only part of wisdom. The other part is everywhere in these volumes, and no reader can miss it. This was written at twenty-eight:

I have moments when all the show around me of shops and streets and conditions generally seems to fade away, and life is seen for what it is, and the main thing to play one's part creditably and haughtily—even with gaiety. . . . Christian philosophers call this wicked pride, but I could respect no one, not even God, if I did not respect myself first.

And this at forty-five:

I am very sorry for your trouble. It doesn't matter where there is courage. I think humility is the solution of almost everything. You can't tell whether you have it, till the time comes. It's a comfort to think that the full enjoyment of life makes for it. Everyone who complains and is disappointed and wronged seems to miss it. It takes something that in some ways is like enormous power of mind (but in others is utterly different) to see things right. The intellectuals fail. The Saints get through quite easy.

Raleigh's Letters

The editorial part of the work has been admirably done. A hurried reading suggests that the text of the letters has been carefully checked. This is important, because in familiar letters anything may be right, so that mistakes elude detection. We have noticed hardly anything that excites suspicion. The footnotes are what they should be—a bare minimum. There is a bibliography, and the informal index is just what is wanted. Mr. Nichol Smith's brief Preface exhibits the judgement and tact to which he has accustomed us. It is tempting to wish that he had let himself go, and risked an estimate of Raleigh's greatness. But doubtless he was right. The verdict is with the future.

Percy and Goldsmith[1]

MISS KATHARINE BALDERSTON, whose edition of Goldsmith's Letters has been announced by the Cambridge University Press, has undertaken two preliminary studies —a census of the manuscripts, which we understand is nearly ready, and the little book before us. The story has been told before, by Goldsmith's biographers; but they did not unfold the whole mystery, partly because they were too easily satisfied, partly because most of the essential documents had disappeared. Miss Balderston has had the luck to find them in London, in the possession of a descendant of Bishop Percy; and she has put the rest of the pieces together from Nichols and the unpublished hoards of

[1] *T.L.S.* 3 June 1926: Review of *The History and Sources of Percy's Memoir of Goldsmith*, by Katharine C. Balderston.

Percy and Goldsmith

American collectors. The result is a good example of the combination of scattered scraps of evidence. It is also exceedingly diverting. The ingredients of a literary farce can seldom have been better mixed.

On 28 April 1773 Dr. Goldsmith, flushed with the triumph of *She Stoops to Conquer*, waited upon Dr. Percy at Northumberland House and dictated to him the story of his life. He also handed over a bundle of documents—'without much inquiry from me at the time, or explanation from him', as Percy confessed later. It consisted chiefly of letters of congratulation about the play; and one may imagine that Goldsmith's best reason for producing it was that he had no other documents to produce. The 'Memoirs from his Own Mouth' Percy worked over from time to time, collecting supplementary information from various quarters, and carefully underlining places where he suspected Goldsmith of embroidery or misremembering.

The intention was, we may suppose, that Percy should be the biographer; but within a few years of Goldsmith's death we find that office assigned to Johnson. Percy handed over his materials; Malone collected others. Whether the Life, and edition of the works, projected by Johnson was an independent affair, or merely part of 'Johnson's Poets', is not quite certain. In any case, it fell through from the contumacy of Carnan, who owned the copyright of *She Stoops*, and was 'a most impracticable man and at variance with all his brethren'. In the face of his opposition, Johnson could do nothing till the copyright should expire in 1787—and then it was too late. Percy, however, thought he had another way open; and within a few months of Johnson's

Percy and Goldsmith

death, having recovered the papers (by a happy accident), he issued proposals in Dublin. But Carnan seems to have threatened proceedings across the Channel; and in 1788 we find Steevens hoping that 'the expiration of the copyright will soon' release the expected work. In 1789 Percy's plans have shifted from Dublin to London, and fresh difficulties begin to show themselves. The Bishop, as he now was, approached John Nichols, who was all compliance: not only would he 'print the work, if your Lordship thinks proper, *meo periculo*'; he would also, 'under your Lordship's assistance, be the ostensible editor'. Why an ostensible editor? Either because Percy thought profane learning inconsonant with the episcopal character, or because he was reluctant to risk further encounters with Ritson. He employed his nephew as ostensible editor of his *Specimens of Blank Verse before Milton*. We do not know why Nichols would not do as publisher, or as ostensible editor. But Percy, having decided on publication in London, seems also to have decided that no business could be transacted but by interview. This may account for the choice of an Irish editor in Thomas Campbell. During the next few years we find Campbell engaged in conscientious efforts to write the life of Goldsmith, whom he had not known, and whose works he had to borrow from the Bishop, not having read them; and both parties making conscientious efforts to meet. In 1791 Percy is in England; Campbell has certified his ability to finish the work *currente prelo* (it is always your most dilatory author who wants the printer to work without supplying him with manuscript). Campbell (though delayed by a lawsuit in Dublin) redoubles his efforts, and arrangements are concerted for his supervising the press in London, while the Bishop corrects the proofs in Bath. But *habent sua fata libelli*—'a delay occurred over the printing', and on 20 June 1795 Campbell died. The 'delay' may have been due to the same inexorable cause, for we learn that 'Mr. Murray of Fleet Street was selected for publisher', and on 6 November 1793 Murray died. In 1795 Percy was in Ireland again, without a publisher, without an ostensible editor.

He did not relinquish the struggle. He entered into negotiations with Cadell and Davies, the obscure course of which was continued during the next few years. Various terms were proposed and accepted, which were subsequently forgotten or misunderstood. The questions whether the publishers should furnish cash—for the benefit of Goldsmith's poor relations—or copies of the work; and, if copies, whether in sheets or stitched in blue paper, and whether saleable in Ireland only or partly also in England, were discussed at intervals. The matter ended with an episcopal memorandum charging the publishers with interpolation, and with refusing to let the author see his own manuscript; and with a 'vindication' published by the other side—doubtless in a periodical of the day, though it has not been recovered. At this point we regret to record that Miss Balderston exhibits signs of impatience. She proves that Cadell and Davies did return part of the manuscript, or a copy of it, for correction; and therefore accuses Percy of forgetfulness, on the ground that there is no evidence of his repeating the application. But what difficulty is there in supposing that he made such application twice, or many times? Chronology does not forbid it; and there might be many things to correct. Besides, by this time the Life had been ostensibly edited by Mr. Boyd, the ingenious translator of Dante, who lived at some distance from Dublin. It does not appear that Boyd did much, though Percy paid him thirty guineas; and it was only natural that, in August, 1797, Percy should call the publishers' attention to the fact that the Life suffered from the circumstance that Boyd was unacquainted with Goldsmith, and that he, Percy, could 'exceedingly improve it, which I am willing to do gratis, and with as much speed as is consistent with my health and other more important engagements, not to mention other avocations'.

The miscellaneous works of Oliver Goldsmith were published in four volumes in 1801. To the edition was prefixed a memoir of the poet. The ostensible editor was Samuel Rose, known to Percy and his friends as the Interpolator. Maurice Goldsmith, for whose benefit the book was planned, had been dead ten years, and his niece, who succeeded to his expectations, did not live to receive anything from the sale of the 250 copies assigned her. Thus this comedy has a tragi-comic underplot.

Aspects of Johnson[1]

MR. HOLLIS'S *American Heresy* has been praised by Mr. Chesterton as 'the wisest and wittiest book that has appeared for some time past'. His essays on Johnson cannot

[1] *T.L.S.* 20 Sept. 1928, 18 Jan. 1934: Reviews of *Dr. Johnson* by Christopher Hollis, Sir Frank MacKinnon's Presidential Address to the Johnson Society of Lichfield, and *Samuel Johnson* by 'Hugh Kingsmill' (H. K. Lunn).

fail to rouse curiosity. He has written a book so readable and interesting that we are sorry he should have written it in a hurry. His quotations are not always strictly relevant, and are often inaccurate. There is some slipshod writing, and a good deal of mere 'cleverality' (the word is Mr. Hollis's). These are perhaps defects of youth and haste. A graver fault is the neglect of an important part of the subject. Whatever Johnson was not, he was assuredly a great scholar and a great critic. Mr. Hollis has not cared to acquaint himself with either aspect of his hero's genius. He quotes from the Dictionary some of the blundering definitions which 'everybody knows', and adds 'there is very little more that is worth knowing'. The late Henry Bradley, a greater philologist than Johnson, recognized him as a pioneer in a difficult branch of science, and spoke with enthusiasm of his rare skill in the choice of illustrative quotations. Mr. Hollis condemns the Dictionary in familiar terms:

> Johnson set out to 'fix' the English language. . . . The task was, in its nature, impossible. Even had it been possible to nature, it would not have been possible to Johnson, for he was no etymologist and knew little of any Elizabethan authors except Shakespeare and Ben Jonson—two fatal handicaps. . . . His ignorance is very clear . . . from the absence of quotation from other authors.

The two specific criticisms here repeated by Mr. Hollis derive from Macaulay. The second is absurdly exaggerated. Johnson's familiarity with Spenser, Bacon, Hooker, and Raleigh is attested by every page of the Dictionary. He 'loved the old black-letter books', and was among the first to point out that an editor of Shakespeare ought to read the books which Shakespeare read. Neither criticism is relevant. Neither ignorance of etymology nor ignorance of Elizabethan literature need have frustrated Johnson's ambition to ascertain the standard of polite usage in the Augustan age.

Mr. Hollis's attitude to that storehouse of wisdom, *The Lives of the Poets*, is equally offhand. He repeats the old story that 'after he received his pension, Johnson's literary activity came almost to an end'. He does indeed mention the political tracts; but he forgets that the *Preface to Shakespeare* and, probably, a large part of the edition itself were written after 1762; he forgets the *Journey to the Western Islands*; and he makes very light of the four substantial volumes of the *Lives*. He describes them as 'trifles'; he supposes that 'they are not much read now'; and there is little reason to believe that he has much read them himself, for almost all the knowledge he betrays of Johnson's literary criticism may have been got from Boswell or from Walter Raleigh's essays. This indifference is due to a preconception. Mr. Hollis has made up his mind that Johnson 'cared nothing for poetry', 'knew little of Shakespeare the poet', 'very imperfectly knew what poetry was'. This 'incapacity' for 'aesthetic appreciation' he in one place ascribes to 'physical defects'; but this is loose thinking. Defects of eye and ear may explain Johnson's indifference to painting and music; but if it is true that 'the window of beauty was a window through which he could never look', it will not do to seek an explanation merely physical. But the premise is false, and it is needless to marshal evidence against it. If Johnson

Aspects of Johnson

had been deaf to the music of Shakespeare he could not have written the *Preface* or the Drury Lane *Prologue*. If admiration for Milton had not been wrung from him by the splendour of Milton's verse, he could not have written the beautiful and noble sentences in praise of Milton which Mr. Hollis quotes.

If this were a catch-penny book it would not deserve careful criticism. But it is much more. When Mr. Hollis is on the themes at which he has worked—Johnson's character, his political and religious convictions, and the inexhaustible treasure of his talk—he is always interesting, and often novel. Johnson, he writes

is not merely handing on as a writer the lesson which he learnt yesterday as a reader. The truth is his own truth. He has discovered it for himself, and the discovery has been none the less real if other wise men have made it before him.

This is well said, and Mr. Hollis deserves the same praise. Many books have been written about Johnson's opinions, but a new one is never unwelcome, so it be acute and honest. Mr. Hollis is sometimes over-confident that he has got Johnson's meaning. But he does not make the mistake of thinking that his meaning is easily grasped. The great Tory is, in fact, still difficult to follow, at least in his talk. Abundant as the evidence for his opinions is, it is unequal in value; it is for the most part fragmentary, and not seldom obscure or conflicting. It is often difficult to discover how far his sayings were wholly serious, how far they were exaggerated, or *ad hominem*, or modified by a lost context. His contemporaries were sometimes at variance in their interpretations; and for us the difficulty is increased by the growing

Aspects of Johnson

obscurity of the social and political background. And though unmatched for the sincerity and directness of his talk, Johnson is far too great to be simple. To 'travel over his mind' is a long and not an easy journey. It was never better worth undertaking than it is today.

'Johnson is known to us as no other great man, either alive or dead, is known.' So Sir Frank MacKinnon recently told the Johnson Society of Lichfield. So we all say, and doubtless it is true. 'The old philosopher is still with us.' But with all our intimacy, can we read him like a book? Macaulay perhaps thought he could. Today we are as far from agreement as were his contemporaries. Allowance must be made for partiality and antipathy; no man is uniformly popular or uniformly estimated. But is there not surprisingly little in common between Boswell's Johnson and Walpole's Johnson? Mrs. Piozzi's Johnson is himself a bundle of contradictions, exhibiting every virtue and almost every contrary vice. That is partly because Mrs. Thrale was 'wiggle-waggle', and did not know a contradiction when she saw one. But it is partly because the subject of her study was beyond her comprehension.

Sir Frank MacKinnon is one of those who think that Boswell did not always understand him either; and that from his excess of reverence (genuine or conventional) he often distorted the course of Johnson's thoughts. Boswell had many motives for his guidance of a conversation, not all of which were disinterested. But certainly his exalted conception of the Rambler made him force Johnson's attention on gloomy topics, often on topics which wearied him. Sir Frank's stout contention that Johnson was 'a much more

Aspects of Johnson

cheerful, more humorous and happier man than Boswell allows' is supported by good witnesses, and is borne out by many of the letters to Mrs. Thrale.

Mr. Kingsmill's able and attractive book is rather a critical study of the subject than an introduction to it. It will not be easily appraised, or always understood, except by those who have some previous acquaintance with Johnsonian literature. Even they will find it hard to test his judgements, from which they are likely often to dissent; for he cites few authorities and gives no references. But the method has the advantage of giving us, in a very manageable book, a clear and vivid picture. Kingsmill's Johnson is a consistent figure. As a study of the essential Johnson the book has great merit. The survey of the evidence, if not exact, is wide; he knows that to get the whole of Johnson we must take account of the *Rambler* and the *Prayers and Meditations* as well as of Boswell and the other anecdotists. He has a just sense of the quality of Johnson's writings. In the analysis of motives Mr. Kingsmill is a modernist whom some readers will find too modern. When Johnson was finishing the Dictionary he wrote to Tom Warton at Oxford:

> I now begin to see land, after having wandered . . . in this vast sea of words. What reception I shall meet with upon the shore I know not . . . whether I shall find upon the coast a Calypso that will court or a Polypheme that will eat me. But if Polypheme comes to me, have at his eyes. I hope however the critics will let me be at peace.

The sustained simile (there is more of it, from Ariosto as well as Homer) may be thought pedantic; but its application is plain. Mr. Kingsmill is not satisfied; he suspects that Johnson was hankering after a second marriage, and says that 'the playful classical allusion (to Calypso) probably concealed a desire which he was half ashamed of'. This is a rare aberration; but Mr. Kingsmill is too prone to ascribe Johnson's words or actions, his silences or inactivities, to repressions and frustrations of sexual or other emotions. That his life was a long frustration is in one sense true; it was indeed spent in contemplating 'that happiness which here I could not find, and that virtue which here I have not attained'. But a character of almost unexampled strength and independence cannot be explained as a complex of negations. Yet no reader can miss the force and sincerity with which Mr. Kingsmill impresses his vision of a lonely and tragic figure:

> Exhausted by his sense of guilt, he abandoned himself to a morbid inertia, from which his sense of guilt would try to raise him, and exhaust him still further. In this vicious circle most of his life was spent. He was bound to what he was attempting to escape. His desire to use his gifts consumed itself in despair that he was neglecting to use them.

This view is powerfully enforced out of Johnson's mouth:

> I was ashamed . . . to find how long and how often I had resolved. . . . Whether I have not lived resolving till the possibility of performance is past, I know not. God help me. I will yet try.

But not even the *Prayers and Meditations* comprehend their author. Johnson, an accomplished writer of dedications, said that 'the known style of dedication is flattery'. He would have said that the proper topic of a Christian's and a sinner's meditation is self-examination and self-abasement. The

Aspects of Johnson

Prayers and Meditations are true; but they are not an autobiography.

If we have indicated a defect in Mr. Kingsmill's thinking, it is not a fatal defect. The aspect of Johnson which his book unfolds is well seen and strongly sketched. It is only not complete. In matters of detail—not always unimportant detail—Mr. Kingsmill's statements must be read with caution. He has no certain grasp of the facts of Johnson's literary career. He tells us that Johnson looked upon his Dictionary 'as a vexatious interruption of his real work'. But what work did it interrupt? Johnson was a journalist and a professional scholar. We know that he 'liked that muddling work'; and we have no good reason to think that he quarrelled with his tasks on the Harleian Catalogue and the like, or that he felt himself shut off by poverty from his true vocation. If he thought of anything as his proper work it was the 'pure wine' of his *Ramblers*, which were actually an interruption of his lexicography. Mr. Kingsmill says the *Rambler* was stopped by 'the necessity to get on with the Dictionary'. There is no evidence for this. The *Rambler* ran to 208 numbers—more than the *Idler* or the *Adventurer*, and the same as the *World*. The *Rambler* was not very successful, and two papers a week may well have exhausted the vein, or the publisher's patience. It is a mistake to think of Johnson as a scholar, an editor, or a critic, against the grain. He shrank from the labour of writing; but he did not despise what he called the 'inferior fame' of a commentator; and only by a strong external impulse was he prompted to a sustained effort of independent composition—by the death of Savage, the death of his mother, a tour to the Hebrides.

Aspects of Johnson

Walter Raleigh was wrong, too, in thinking that the Dictionary 'might have been successfully carried through by a merely mechanical genius'. His own age had a truer instinct. Johnson was a pioneer in lexicography, and the great compilation has the marks of no mechanical genius.

The biography of Johnson may borrow a hint from his iconography. There are many portraits of Johnson by Reynolds and others. All are unmistakably Johnson. Yet they differ from one another in a very unusual degree. Perhaps the right frontispiece for Mr. Kingsmill's book was not the placid, kindly old man whom Reynolds saw in his last years, but that earlier portrait by Reynolds of a man with clenched fingers and an expression of tortured strength. Johnson's character and genius are, and must remain, enigmatical. They are everywhere recognizable, but they will not be defined. Of all his qualities that which most rivets the attention is his inexhaustible versatility.

Boswell without Johnson[1]

USING the style of 'The Hypochondriack' Boswell contributed a series of seventy essays to the *London Magazine*. They appeared monthly without interruption for nearly six years, 1777–83. A design of republication is hinted in the concluding number, and is perhaps reflected in a well-known episode told in the *Life* under 1783:

---

[1] *T.L.S.* 6 Sept. 1928: Review of Boswell's *The Hypochondriack*, edited by Margery Bailey.

Boswell without Johnson

I told him I should send him some *Essays* which I had written, which I hoped he would be so good as to read, and pick out the good ones. *Johnson.* 'Nay, Sir, send me only the good ones; don't make *me* pick them.'

This has been taken to mean that Johnson discouraged the idea of a book. If he did so, we need not suppose that he read the essays and thought meanly of them, or that without reading them he distrusted Boswell's powers. He had praised the Corsican journal; and in 1773 the manuscript journal of the Hebridean tour had opened his eyes to Boswell's gift of writing. It is more probable that he disliked the subject, or rather the title—for the topic of melancholy is not really very prominent in *The Hypochondriack*. That Boswell seriously entertained the design is now certain. The collection preserved at Malahide, and recently acquired by Colonel Isham, contains a file of the first forty numbers, prepared by Boswell for a collected edition. That Boswell should form and relinquish such a plan will surprise no one who remembers the imposing catalogue of the literary projects which he did not complete, nor so far as is known even begin. It is much more surprising that he should have written the *Hypochondriacks* with a punctuality so long sustained than that he should have failed to republish them, occupied as he was, from the end of 1784 or earlier, with *Tour* and *Life*.

The *Hypochondriacks*, then, remained uncollected—as good as buried in the files of the *London Magazine*. With the growth of Boswell's literary reputation, people began to collect his minor or non-Johnsonian books and pamphlets, and (more rarely) to read in them. *Corsica* was reprinted, the letters adequately edited. An edition of the *Hypochondriacks* was prepared by Mr. A. W. Evans, and was actually in type; but their ill luck held: the type was consumed by a fire at the printer's. Meantime it became known that an edition on a more elaborate plan was preparing in America. Mr. Evans (who has already found time in his life for more careers than one) bowed to destiny; and Dr. Margery Bailey's edition enters the arena alone. Boswell Redux, Boswell Redivivus—it makes a fine show, in two handsome volumes admirably printed, with all the panoply of critical introduction, elaborate commentary, full-dress index, and an emblematic binding of black and silver.

If Boswell's genius has been obscured by a century of hostility and ignorance, there is now a danger lest it be smothered by the enthusiasm of his admirers. If Boswell had reprinted these essays, we suppose they would have made two volumes duodecimo, and it is safe to assert that they would have enjoyed considerable popularity; but 700 pages large octavo, and fifteen dollars, may be too severe a handicap. There is nothing to be said against Dr. Bailey's commentary—it is learned, accurate, and judicious—except that it makes it exceedingly difficult to read the text. It is a hard case, for it must be allowed that the text bristles with temptations—classical quotations and allusions, echoes of Johnson's talk and writings, parallels unnumbered with the *Life* and the letters. Dr. Bailey surrenders, more than willingly, to every temptation; and the result of her tireless devotion is to make her idol look rather foolish. The slender fabric of occasional journalism is not equal to such a load. It was a case, we think, for heroic restraint. Perhaps the notes should not have been printed on the same page with the text.

We hasten to add (risking consistency) that the notes in themselves are good reading. The introduction is much more than readable: it is packed with knowledge, and gives a temperate and sympathetic estimate of Boswell's literary character. That his character will be raised by the rediscovery of these essays need not be doubted. If we are to consider Boswell as a man of letters, counting out the *Tour* and the *Life* (in which he shines, however brightly, in the reflected blaze of a larger luminary), the *Hypochondriacks* must be reckoned his most important published work. They are not the equal of his letters, but that was not to be expected. Boswell is doubtless telling the truth when he says that they were written when he had 'just time to do them with rapid agitation'; and is probably sincere in speaking of them as journalistic trifles by which he set no great store. But they are surprisingly good; 'independent and sincere, dignified without stiffness, and gay without frivolity', as their editor justly and happily claims; more serious, more coherent, and better-informed than accords with the common notion of Boswell's nature, yet not without many flashes of his inimitable naivety.

The Hypochondriack establishes what was always probable, that Boswell's melancholia was a real affliction, and not a foolish fancy. Johnson may have thought it affectation; or he may have thought his friend young enough, and healthy enough, to be laughed and scolded into serenity. Certainly he disliked the topic, which he had too much reason to shun and of which Boswell was immoderately fond. It might well have been of Death and Melancholy that he told Boswell, 'Sir, you have but two subjects, and I am sick of both.'

Boswell without *Malone*[1]

THE publication of Boswell's *Archives at Auchinleck* proceeds with regularity and dispatch, and it is now possible to survey the performance of the American scholars to whom fate has committed it. When Colonel Isham bore off the prize from Malahide Castle, he resolved on the speedy publication of a plain text of Boswell's journals in a limited and sumptuous edition, and chose as editor the late Geoffrey Scott, an Englishman (nephew of Scott of the *Manchester Guardian*), who had already flirted with Boswellian studies in his accomplished biography of *Zélide*. Scott quickly got to work, and had published six volumes before his sudden untimely death. He was almost inevitably succeeded by Professor Pottle of Yale, whose elaborate bibliography of Boswell's published writings had broken fresh ground in the use of bibliographical evidence for the purposes of biography. Professor Pottle drove the work to a triumphant conclusion in 1934, when the last of eighteen volumes appeared (folio and quarto). This series gave us the major part of Boswell's finished journals, and his rough notes when the finished journals had never been written or were

---

[1] *T.L.S.* 7 Nov. 1936: Review of *Boswell's Journal of a Tour to the Hebrides with Samuel Johnson, LL.D.* Now first published from the original manuscript. Edited by Frederick A. Pottle and Charles H. Bennett.

Boswell without Malone

missing, together with many letters and other relevant documents. Meanwhile Professor Pottle had issued (with his wife's help) a succinct Catalogue of the Malahide Papers, and he has since completed an elaborate index to the eighteen volumes, which is being printed at Oxford.

The *Private Papers*, which would fill a large shelf, if any shelf could receive their various bulk, can hardly as yet be said to have become public. In this country few sets are available; of those few most are due to Colonel Isham's munificence. The index, indeed, will have a much wider circulation, and will dispense scholars from the necessity of perusing the volumes in a public library and of making their own notes.

But all this, however imposing, is no more than the overture. For both the scholar and the common reader much more is in store. Professor Pottle and his collaborators at Yale are already at work on a complete edition of the journals, which will do for them what Birkbeck Hill and Dr. Powell have done (or are doing) for Boswell's published works and the other Johnsoniana. This must be the labour of many years. But we are promised at no great distance a popular edition. This has been undertaken by an enterprising and (in this connexion) well-named New York publishing firm, the Viking Press. It is understood that this edition will be in four volumes (but see below!) and will contain all Boswell's completed journals, with a light commentary. Finally it is believed that Professor Pottle, whose powers as a writer have been shown in his prefaces, designs a life of Boswell.

The publication in 1931 of the Pottle Catalogue of the

Boswell without Malone

Papers revealed a discrepancy between the edition as planned (and then nearing completion, apart from its index) and the manuscripts which it represented. There had been a further find in 1930, of which the chief treasure was the journal of the Hebridean tour. Colonel Isham had already given or promised his subscribers more than full measure, and could not be asked to add another bulky journal. There were, moreover, difficulties of time and of plan; the editor had already passed 1773, and this was not in the full sense an unpublished journal.

The edition now published fills this gap, and bridges in a convenient way the gulf between the *Private Papers* and the popular edition which is in prospect. The limited edition (now before us) matches, though modest in octavo, the eighteen volumes of the *Private Papers*, already reinforced by the octavo Catalogue and soon to be equipped with an octavo index. The 'trade' edition, to be published in the spring of 1937 at a guinea, will be the forerunner of the popular edition, but will ultimately form its fifth volume. There is happily no competition between the new 'Hebrides' and the fifth volume of Hill's Boswell—that is the *Tour* as published in 1785—now under revision by Dr. Powell. Pottle's edition gives the reader clear indications of the differences between the journal and the published *Tour*, but makes no attempt to edit the text of 1785 as such. The curious reader may easily compare the two versions. Powell's edition, with its much fuller commentary, is thus not forestalled; but it will take account of the original version only as it explains errors or obscurities of 1785. The two editors have been in communication throughout, and have freely

Boswell without Malone

exchanged their stores. But the debt of Oxford to Yale is of necessity by far the greater.

The manuscript which is the basis of the new edition consisted of about 675 pages, of which about 600 survive. Boswell began in earnest when the travellers left Edinburgh on 18 August 1773 and ended at Lochbuie on 22 October. He took two notebooks, got a third from Johnson in Skye, and bought some loose sheets at the shop in Col. He made rough notes for the next few days, and these he wrote up in 1779 and later, so completing the journal which was read by Johnson, Forbes, and Mrs. Thrale. In 1785, when publication became possible, Boswell composed an introduction and conclusion and, with Malone's constant aid, drastically reduced and revised the whole. For reduction Boswell had two good reasons. One was a matter of bulk. The first edition exceeds 500 pages. Further, what Boswell offered was *The Journal of a Tour in the Hebrides with Samuel Johnson, LL.D.* Modesty dictated the suppression of experiences and speculations in which Johnson had no share. But there were other motives. Boswell, who knew what he could do well, was diffident of his powers as a topographer, or as what was soon afterwards called a picturesque writer. He had little taste for scenery. 'I find a wretched deficiency in expressing visible objects.' As a conscientious diarist he put it in, but he was not unwilling to take it out.

There were also questions of delicacy. The primitive sanitation of the Hebrides afforded poignant experiences, and was inevitably matter of discussion and speculation. This could not be printed. Nor could a reverent public be informed that Johnson had called the Rev. Kenneth Macaulay

Boswell without Malone

'the grossest bastard'. The editors are for the present content to tell us that the reading of the manuscript is here certain. Perhaps we may assume that 'bastard' is not a mere term of abuse, but a metaphor alluding to Johnson's and Boswell's belief that Macaulay had not written a book published with his name. But that Johnson was capable of coarse language need surprise no one now; indeed, the news will be generally welcomed.

Mr. Macaulay was not the only person on whom the traveller's displeasure fell. The altercations with Sir Alexander Macdonald and his lady set the manners of the age—alike of hosts and guests—in a striking light. Even after revision and the later cancellation of a leaf, the printed record nearly led to a duel, and did lead to further suppression in the second edition.

When all allowance has been made, most readers will accept the editors' judgement that Malone's regard for propriety, elegance, and correct English led him further than Boswell was always willing to follow. Malone held the pen—most of the revision is in his hand—and that was decisive. It was he, we need not doubt, who generalized the bill of fare, a piece of journalism that has made Woodforde's reputation and will not hurt Boswell's. In one place his reluctance shows itself in a wistful query—'Shall the dinner *stet*?' It was 'mutton-chops, a broiled chicken, and bacon and eggs, and a bottle of Malaga'.

The upshot of it all is that the Johnsonian, as such, will be a little disappointed, if his expectations were high. Boswell and Malone knew how to present Johnson, and their redaction did him little harm. But the Boswellian will de-

Boswell without Malone

light in the undress of a journal written at heat by a Boswell who was young and vigorous, happily married, sober (on the whole) and virtuous, enjoying his richest and purest experience. The weather was atrocious, and Johnson was sometimes deaf and out of temper. But they both loved the Islanders, and the Islanders them, at sight. 'Wherever we have come, we have been received like princes in their progress.'

The editors make light of the difficulties of their task. The original journal, when Mrs. Thrale read it, was no doubt very easy. But the deletions and interlineations of 1785, and the later ravages of damp, have turned it into a palimpsest. None of these difficulties is allowed to vex the reader. We cannot praise too highly the courage and good sense of the editors, who have imposed on themselves no rigid rules. Thus they restore the manuscript text (often in silence if restoration is certain) from the printed *Tour*, following the first edition as presumably closest to the manuscript. On the other hand, the introduction and conclusion, composed in 1785, are printed from Boswell's third edition, because that had his final approval. The footnotes which Boswell added in 1785 or 1786 were of considerable bulk and varying relevance; Boswell lost his sense of proportion when he came to edit himself. The editors have used these notes, or discarded them, at discretion. The book is beautifully printed by Mr. Updike and has some tantalizing facsimiles.

Johnson and Queeney[1]

SINCE Johnson's letters were first collected, forty years ago, by Dr. Birkbeck Hill many new letters, important and unimportant, have come to light. Hill supposed that the letters to Perkins had been refused to Boswell, as they were refused to himself, and feared that 'perhaps a second hundred years must pass away before it shall be ascertained what was the part that Johnson took in founding the new firm of Barclay and Perkins'. These letters survive in a family collection. Boswell had seen them, and returned them, for the most part unused. They consist largely of intimations that the supply of coals in Bolt-court was running low. The letters to Dr. Taylor, which *were* denied to Boswell, had been widely scattered; but few of them now remain untraced. Some twenty letters to Chambers, Chief Justice of Bengal, have come back from India, bearing the marks of a long sojourn in the East, but still legible. Only the other day a number of letters to Mrs. Thrale, not included by Mrs. Piozzi in her collection, were acquired by the Rylands Library of Manchester.

But these recoveries, and many more in the same field, are far outshone by Lord Lansdowne's recent find. The great intrinsic value of this cache is enhanced by its romantic history. Johnson's correspondence with Hester Maria Thrale, whom he called his Queeney, was known from allusions in his letters to her mother. But when Mrs. Piozzi in

[1] *T.L.S.* 13 Mar. 1932: Review of *Johnson and Queeney*, letters edited by the sixth Marquis of Lansdowne.

Johnson and Queeney

1788 published 'Letters to and from the late Samuel Johnson' she printed no letters to Queeney, though she printed five to Susannah and one to Sophia. It was alleged by Baretti (a doubtful authority) that Miss Thrale 'refused to give up' Johnson's letters 'when her mother applied for them'. We now know that Mrs. Piozzi did try to get these letters, and (to do her justice) that she appreciated their worth. Lord Lansdowne is allowed to quote from 'Thraliana' an entry (not quoted by Hayward in his 'Autobiography of Mrs. Piozzi') of 1 May 1787: 'Johnson's letters are at Press—may they succeed! if my eldest daughter would have given me hers from him, how it would have helped the Compilation!'

Queeney kept her letters close; unlike Susannah's, they show little sign of handling. Their ultimate discovery is the result of family history. The four Thrale girls who survived childhood lived to a combined age of 314. Susannah, Queeney's most dangerous rival for Johnson's heart ('I was always a Susy when nobody else was a Susy'), never changed her name, and at eighty-seven was described as 'a comfortable old lady full of good works', but not of literary tastes; 'she does not care to talk about Dr. Johnson, and still less about her mother.' Her sisters married; but they left only one descendant, Queeney's only daughter, and their personal possessions were reassembled in her person. This was Georgina Elphinstone, daughter of Admiral Lord Keith, who married Queeney when she was forty-three, being then a widower with a grown-up daughter. The admiral died at his house in Scotland in 1823; his widow lived until 1858—the last survivor of the persons named by Boswell. Their daughter became Mrs. John Villiers, and later Lady William

Osborne. She, like Johnson, 'rode harder at a fox-chase than anyone', and was known to her intimates as Aunt Jack; but she does not concern us otherwise than as the heiress of all manner of Thraliana, which at her death in 1892 passed to the representative of her father's elder daughter (by the former marriage), the late Marquis of Lansdowne.

Johnson 'was at a certain period of his life a good deal with the Earl of Shelburne' (less well known as first Marquess of Lansdowne); and Shelburne when Prime Minister rented Streatham Park. These facts have nothing to do with the present story; and scholars are as a rule sadly ignorant of the mazes of the 'Peerage'. So the Johnsonian world had never thought of Bowood as a Mecca, or as a quarry. Yet there is the baptismal basin of Mrs. Thrale's Welsh ancestors, and the portrait by Zoffany of her mother, Mrs. Salusbury (and of the dog Belle, who ate Johnson's toast); there are Reynolds's ravishing picture of Queeney herself, and Cosway's miniature of the lovely Susannah; there are Queeney's cabinet, Johnson's gift, and books given to her and her sisters by Johnson, Percy, and Baretti; there are 350 letters to Queeney from her mother; there is 'Aunt Jack', the last of the Thrales, in the costume of a Victorian *equestrienne*; and there, recently extricated from a mass of family papers, are Johnson's letters to his favourite, thirty-two in number.

No editor of Thralian documents can escape the controversy about Mrs. Thrale's second marriage. The verdict of her contemporaries is notorious. Malone, a temperate and charitable man, called her 'this abandoned woman'. There has been a strong reaction, and nearly all recent writers on

Johnson and Queeney

Mrs. Piozzi may be called her apologists. Lord Lansdowne's judgement, though more candid than Malone's, is severe. He finds her 'a woman essentially vain, vulgar, and false, intolerable as a parent and rightly kept at a distance by her offspring'. He will perhaps be suspected of taking sides—Queeney's against her mother. But the condemnation of her behaviour at the time was almost unanimous, and the explanations of this offered by modern apologists were never quite convincing. Lord Lansdowne's conclusion, moreover, is not hastily reached; for he has read not only a great deal of unpublished correspondence in his own archives (this will be the matter of a further volume), but also the six quarto volumes of 'Thraliana' which are now in the great Huntington library and will presently be published.

But this is at best a tiresome business. We are glad to turn to the letters and to rejoice that their owner has given us this jewel by itself, very little 'clouded by incrustations' or 'debased by impurities' of a rather sordid and saddening story. The gem shines all the brighter for its gay setting of portraits, cabinets, baptismal basins, and other relics, reproductions of which embellish this volume. The next editor of Johnson's letters will be proud to place these in their chronological order with the rest; but then they will mix with the world, with 'a mass of meaner minerals', and must lose some of the beauty which comes of isolation.

They are the letters of an elderly man to a child—the first was written before Queeney was seven—or of an old man to a girl—the last was written before she was twenty. The serenity of this communion of wisdom with innocence is somewhat clouded by pain and mortality, but is unvexed by petty ills, and is everywhere radiant with the tenderest solicitude. The letters are nicely accommodated to the age and tastes of his correspondent; but he does not insult her by any departure from his natural modes of thought and expression. 'I have been very grave, but you are a very thinking Lady.' 'This, my lovely Dear, is a very grave and long lesson, but do not think it tedious.' So the language has that accuracy, the rhythm those melodies, which we have learned to expect:

> You, dear Madam, I suppose wander philosophically by the seaside, and survey the vast expanse of the world of waters, comparing as your predecessors in contemplation have done its ebb and flow, its turbulence and tranquility, to the vicissitudes of human life.

The letters abound in good advice. There are sermons against idleness, against sulking ('Never delight yourself with the dignity of silence or the superiority of inattention'), against illegibility: exhortations in favour of reading, of activity, and of course of arithmetic: disquisitions, serious and playful, on a camp ('the real scene of heroick life'), on the pleasures of novelty, on ventriloquy and on balloons. Of these the praise of arithmetic is perhaps the most moving, the warning against illegibility the most cogent, the essay on camps the most entertaining. But surely the most spirited is this dissuasive against idleness:

> If ever therefore you catch yourself contentedly and placidly doing nothing, *sors de l'enchantement*, break away from the snare, find your book or your needle, or snatch the broom from the maid.

Johnson and Queeney

We need not wonder that the owner of these letters chose to keep them from profane eyes. But now that they have lain hidden, perhaps for more than a century, we need not scruple to share her pleasure.

Jane Austen[1]

JANE AUSTEN or Miss Austen? The question is much canvassed. 'Miss Austen' is no doubt a tribute of delicacy to a lady who unmistakably and essentially was a lady, as Horace Walpole was a gentleman. We do not much inquire whether Samuel Johnson was a gentleman, or Emily Brontë a lady. Perhaps it is a similar sentiment that prompts us still sometimes to say Mr. Pope, or Mr. Pitt, or Mr. Gladstone. The last generation regularly said Miss Edgeworth, and even Miss Burney. We still say Miss Ferrier (if we say anything), having forgotten her Christian name. But at this distance of time there is no impropriety, nor even 'inelegance', in anyone's saying 'Jane Austen'. Those who are admitted to her private life, in Hampshire and Kent and London, will feel even a certain awkwardness in giving her a title she would hardly have recognized as hers. 'Miss Austen' was, of course, her elder sister.

Jane Austen, then, and (perhaps) Sir Walter Scott are the only pre-Victorian English novelists who are still popular. We claim a general familiarity with the novelists of the

---

[1] *Time and Tide*, 27 July 1935: Review of *Jane Austen* by Lord David Cecil.

preceding age. But the *Vicar* and *Tom Jones* are a habit with few of us. Jane Austen has lasted even better than Scott, for Scott has become a costume author. But the schoolgirl who picks up *Pride and Prejudice* will probably class it with other 'pre-war' fiction. She may notice the absence of railways, and a certain precision of language. I doubt if she is at all aware of a gulf of 120 years.

Jane Austen's genius has placed her among the fixed stars, whose light time does not dim. But she has had to wait for critical appraisement. Her family and other contemporaries left some ejaculations of affectionate admiration. Coleridge praised her 'genuine and individual productions'. Scott made two notes in his journals, one of 'the exquisite touch which renders commonplace characters interesting from the truth of the description and the sentiment', the other of this author's incomparable gift of 'finishing off'. Later, Macaulay printed his famous eulogy and Charlotte Brontë made her famous demurrer. But to the Victorians, generally, Jane Austen was a reader's rather than a critic's novelist. She was read for entertainment, but did not seem very important. In our own time she has become a touchstone. But her detractors have, perhaps, had rather the best of the debate. Walter Raleigh, however, in his early book on the novel, gave the right answer to a vexed question: 'the world of pathos and passion is present in her work by implication.' Recently, there have been some good special studies, notably Lord David's own of *Sense and Sensibility*, and Miss Mary Lascelles's of *Mansfield Park*. But the present essay is the best general account of the matter, perhaps the first that can be called adequate to its subject.

Jane Austen

Lord David's history is not equal to his criticism. He has not got the picture of Jane Austen's life quite in focus, and he betrays himself by slips in matter of fact. Thus, he repeats the legend of a 'small parsonage house' as her workshop. In fact, she left her father's parsonage when she was about five-and-twenty, and a parsonage was never again her home. Lord David's description of her time as mostly spent 'in the drawing-room, sewing and gossiping' does less than justice to the variety of her experience. She sewed, of course, and she sometimes did the housekeeping. But as a rule she was spared such avocations, and it is clear, I think, that from an early age she was regarded in her family as rarely endowed, and entitled to such privileges as they could give her. I do not mean that her writing was made an excuse for neglecting the obvious duties of life: the duties of a churchwoman, of a daughter, a sister, and—most onerous of all—an aunt; for she was a multifarious aunt. But she had more leisure and more scope, especially in London and at Godmersham, than is allowed for; more time, particularly, for reading and for talk about books. Lord David remarks that 'her range of character is very large'. The range of character is actually larger in her letters than in the novels; and the life revealed in the letters gave her abundant material for study.

But this is almost (not quite) unimportant. It has not prevented Lord David from saying the right things, and leaving nothing essential unsaid. He will not think this grudging praise; it is as much as Jane Austen could have given him.

She is the most satisfactory of English novelists, he tells

us, in the first place because 'she stays within the range of her imaginative inspiration'. This restraint enabled her to produce books which are almost free from padding and vamping. That her vision is limited, because it leaves out God and politics, is not to say that it is narrow or of second-rate interest. Lord David avoids the common mistake of making such an admission. 'A man's relation to his wife and children is at least as important a part of his life as his relation to his beliefs and career; and reveals him as fundamentally.' Secondly, we must remember that she is a comedian, limited in her imaginative inspiration to a literary convention which she never deserts. Thirdly, she is a moralist and a realist. 'The issues between Elinor and Marianne are the issues between Rousseau and Dr. Johnson.' If we grasp these essentials as Lord David has grasped them, we shall be in no danger of repeating the old silly complaints that Jane Austen tells us nothing about the Battle of Waterloo. We shall be free to enjoy what she does give us, and to appreciate its profound moral and artistic sensibility.

If I have a misgiving, it concerns those of her critics who are not free to enjoy Jane Austen, or not without reservations, though they are constrained to admit her genius. Lord David has a short way with these surly fellows; there are people, he says, 'who do not like sunshine or unselfishness'. I wish I found it as easy as that. There are, of course, and will always be people whom Jane Austen does not amuse, because they are stupid. Some of these were among her acquaintance, as she records for her own amusement and ours. But there are perverse people who can admire Jane Austen without liking her. I think it is their fault not hers; but I know some of them too well to set them down as morose or uncharitable.

This inquiry would take me too far, and I am not sure of my direction. But for the much larger class of Jane Austen's readers, whose enjoyment is unalloyed by any scruples, Lord David's summation may be commended as the best we have and as all we need ask. His essay is full of brave words. 'It was wrong to marry for money, but it was silly to marry without it.' Jane Austen has been refused credit for the first of these beliefs, and scolded for the second. Most of us hold them both, but hesitate to applaud a writer who voices them. Lord David does not find Jane Austen's position cynical or prim. He submits it to the touchstone of his own conduct, declaring that if his behaviour were in question, Jane Austen is the judge whose praise or blame he should most welcome or most dread. The opinion of Balzac or Dickens would carry little weight; but 'I should be seriously upset if I incurred the disapproval of Jane Austen'.

Few judgements of Jane Austen have become, or deserve to become, familiar quotations. This has a better chance than most.

To What Strange Shores?[1]

And do not thou contemn this swelling tide,
   And stream of words, that now doth rise so high
Above the usual banks, and spreads so wide
   Over the borders of antiquity:
Which, I confess, comes ever amplify'd
   With th' abounding humours that do multiply.
. . . .
And who (in time) knows whither we may vent
   The treasure of our tongue? To what strange shores
This gain of our best glory shall be sent
   T' enrich unknowing nations with our stores?
What worlds in th' yet unformed occident,
   May come refin'd with th' accents that are ours?
                      1599, S. DANIEL, *Musophilus*.

SIR WILLIAM CRAIGIE, it has been well said, bestrides the Atlantic like a Colossus. Trained in the severe school of the *New English Dictionary*, that Scots College in Oxford, he became in time its senior editor. But his level eye scanned farther horizons. While still active in editing the *Oxford Dictionary*, and increasing the fine confusion of its Supplement with rich cargoes of *Americana*, he had already transferred his flag to Chicago and fired American scholars with the ambition to renew the Oxford discipline on American soil. The work of collection began in 1925; and it is a great achievement that within a decade materials have been so far amassed and arranged that *A–Baggage*, the first of some

[1] *T.L.S.* 10 Oct. 1936: Review of *A Dictionary of American English on Historical Principles*, edited by Sir William Craigie, with the collaboration of James R. Hulbert. Part I: A–Baggage; and *The American Language*, by H. L. Mencken. Fourth Edition, Corrected, Enlarged, and Rewritten.

To What Strange Shores?

twenty parts, lies before us complete, covering this section of the American alphabet, over three centuries, in 232 closely printed columns. Credit will rightly be given to Sir William and his colleague of the Oxford staff, Mr. George Watson, for their *perfervidum ingenium Scotorum*, and to Oxford for what they carried thence. But it is due also to the University of Chicago for seeing the light, to Mr. James Hulbert of that University, the collaborator, to Mr. Mitford Mathews and Mr. Allen Read, assistant editors, to the noble army of volunteer collectors, and to the General Education Board and other bodies which provided the necessary funds, doubtless with an ample flow.

The plan of the work is very briefly set out in a general preface; this is somewhat expanded in a separate prospectus and in a prefatory note which surveys the contents of Part I. The editors are, perhaps, sanguine in their belief that by observing the symbols they employ 'the reader will learn at a glance some of the essential facts'. Many users of dictionaries make shift to get along without attention to symbols. But this dictionary is of a special type, and without due attention to the symbols may easily mislead. The chief symbols are these. When a word is in English before 1600, and therefore *could* not be an Americanism, it is asterisked. When a word or a sense is certainly, or almost certainly, of American origin it is shown by a plus sign + to be 'an addition to the common language'. The two symbols may be combined in one article; thus *Bee will be followed by + *bee-line*; for though the Englishman's fly, as an Indian called it, was an importation, the *bee-line* was a product of American observation. *Aboard is followed by + *all aboard*,

To What Strange Shores?

* *Around* by the definitions + *here and there at random* ('travel around'), + *to a thing needing to be dealt with* ('things I haven't got around to'), + *through the round of a number of persons* ('not enough to go around'), and other uses of *around* (Eng. *round*). These symbols deal with the more obvious cases—words of American origin and American adaptations of English words.

But often it is not so simple as that. It is a commonplace that many uses have survived in America which in England are obsolete or survive only in dialect (*dove* for *dived* is an example recently debated in these columns). These are Americanisms, though not of American origin. Sometimes it is doubtful whether an American use is imported or invented, since the evidence may be imperfect. In such cases the editors give the English date within {distinctive brackets}, and leave the inference to the intelligent reader. If the question is of priority, the important English date is the earliest. Thus *American*, in the sense of American Indian, is found in England in 1578, in America not until 1641. If it is a question of survival, the important English date is the latest. Thus the transitive use of the verb *appeal* in the legal sense ('the case was appealed to a higher Court') is found in England as late as 1590, but has long been obsolete. In America it survived, or was reborn, and is in everyday use. The editors are rightly cautious in claiming American origin for doubtful cases. Even when the earliest American quotation is earlier than the earliest English quotation they sometimes believe 'that the sense is not (or is not with certainty) of American origin', and the hall-mark + is not assigned.

To What Strange Shores?

But to appreciate the plan of such a work it is necessary to consider its scope. 'A complete historical dictionary of American English would include . . . every word which has been current . . . from the time when the first English-speaking colonists settled on these shores.' But it was seen that so ambitious an undertaking would mean many years of collection and many more of digestion. Moreover a dictionary on such a plan would largely overlap both the *Oxford Dictionary*—which already gives the historical or literary student much of what he needs—and such admirable books as the latest 'Webster', with their vast accumulations of technical words. The promoters accordingly decided to limit themselves to what they regard as distinctively American. Mr. Mencken's less systematic collection, the sustained thesis of which is the superiority of twentieth-century American English to its British cousin, follows in part the same method of exhibiting the differences between the two idioms. Again, practical considerations have compelled the editors of *D.A.E.* to exclude everything which made its first appearance after 1900. The limitation will disappoint many amateurs of the tempo of modern American life, and its 'riproarious' verbal expression. But we may console ourselves with the reflection that the vocabulary before 1900 gives a more coherent and perhaps a more attractive picture than the modern phantasmagoria, which besides may be studied in many existing works.

D.A.E., then, is in the main a dictionary of Americanisms; that is, 'of words or phrases which are clearly or apparently of American origin, or have (strictly it should be 'have or

To What Strange Shores?

have had'?) greater currency here.' But the editors have naturally wished to put before their readers a more complete and lively picture of American life during three centuries than a mere dictionary of differences could give. They have included accordingly 'every word denoting something which has a real connexion (the prospectus has "a clear connexion") with the development of the country and the history of its people.' This principle cannot have been easy of application; and its adoption may make the book more difficult in use. The symbols described above are not a universal test, and we confess ourselves not always perfectly clear on which of the several grounds a word has been included. Our guess is that *acorn* owes its inclusion to its use as a food; *acre* to the odd forms *acker*, *aker*, &c.; *appeal*, the intransitive verb ('to apply to a higher tribunal'), to the existence of the transitive use, noted above as American. The long articles on *agriculture* and its compounds are no doubt due to the importance of agriculture in American life. *Actor* and *actress* have presumably the same justification; but we do not find *acrobat*. *Almond* and *actuary* are puzzling to a layman; and we suspect that *alderman* may puzzle or even mislead some American readers. The English reader, studying the quotations, will make out that American aldermen are popularly elected and that they sometimes form a separate council. An American, innocent of English local government, may wonder if the English alderman is obsolete, or of restricted currency. These difficulties, if they are not imaginary, might very easily be dispelled. Under *acclimate* we find a note: 'Originally English, 1792–1859, but superseded by *acclimatize*, 1836,' and

To What Strange Shores?

all is plain. We would plead for a more frequent relaxation of editorial austerity.

It may confidently be assumed that within the limits imposed *D.A.E.* is virtually complete. We miss *afterward*, which though not classed as obsolete in the *Oxford Dictionary* (*c.* 1888) is surely obsolete in England now, and as surely current in the U.S. We do not find it in Mencken, or in Mr. Horwill's *Modern American Usage*; but it is noted in Fowler's *Modern English Usage*. The transitive verb *accent*, used figuratively where we almost always prefer *accentuate*, is in Horwill ('Lack of money accents every other distress'), not in *D.A.E.* For *put across* we must probably await *put*. *All of* is illustrated in 'all of six feet high', but not in the common, but un-English, use 'all of the words'. 'You can't fool all of the people all of the time.' *Ascension* of a balloon, or of a politician to power, is hardly English, but is not noticed, though apparently common in U.S. Under *around* there is a general note 'frequently employed in place of Eng. round'; but though numerous colloquial phrases are illustrated, as 'not enough to go around', there seems to be no mention of the regular use seen in 'he turned around and went home', or (Horwill) 'the little church around the corner'. The common American pronunciation of *address* (accented on the first syllable) is not noted. Is *ash-can* (our *dust-bin*) later than 1900?

But the interest of this great Thesaurus is hardly affected by such cavil. It is true of this, as of all English dictionaries, that 'by far the greater number of words beginning with A are of an abstract character'; and our survey is limited to that initial. The juicier crop of *B–Baggage* may properly

To What Strange Shores?

be left to the happy reviewer who will enjoy the full bloom of that boisterous initial, luxuriating in booms and bosses, backwoods and back logs, baby-carriages and baggage-tabs. Our concern is rather with accessions and amendments, aboriginals and aliens, apartments and avenues—though even we have apple-jack. By the happiest of accidents we have America herself. In *America*, with its derivatives and its innumerable compounds—from the American Eagle to the American goldfinch—the editors have found the severest test of their skill in marshalling the unruly host, and their most splendid opportunity of showing forth the New World in a verbal microcosm.

The limitation of *America* to the British Colonies of North America is first recorded in 1650, when Mistris Anne Bradstreet was 'residing in America, alias Nov-Anglia'. By 1708 the poet Tompson could describe the Illustrious Winthrop as

> the third of a renowned line
> Which we Americans deemed next divine.

The term was continued to the United States; and it was remarked in 1791 that this 'may have come into use as being much shorter to say *Americans* than citizens of the United States. Some use Atlantic America, others United America—the last is the most proper.' Time has rejected these alternatives—did anyone ever say United Stater?—and the editors confirm the explantion given in 1791. Washington in 1796 saw that 'the name of American . . . must always exalt the just pride of patriotism, more than appellatives derived from local discriminations'.

The earlier sense, an aboriginal American, began in

To What Strange Shores?

England (1578). In the seventeenth century the settlers were exercised by the spiritual darkness of 'those silly seduced Americans'. But by 1752 'the aboriginal Americans have no honesty', and their name was confiscated, so that they had to be qualified as 'aboriginal' or 'native'. As early as about 1650 we hear of 'our American creed', and Mr. Tompson (our poetical friend) was 'that American pillar'. The application gradually hardened, so that by 1847 it was possible to distinguish the 'American' from the 'Canadian' coast of Lake Superior.

We may watch, as in a movie, the development of the national character, language, literature. In 1803 'Our wealth, our power, and our resources are the boast of every American'. In 1808 Napoleon told the American Minister 'that we are very good Americans'. In 1825 an American was 'one of that singular people, who know a little, and but a little, of everything'. In 1861 'The women of America, my boy, are a credit to the America [*sic*] eagle'. By 1873 'Americans must be Americans, and blow up as a necessity of their existence'.

American English is in 1740 'the American Dialect'. But by 1789 Webster was concerned to 'preserve the purity of the American tongue', and in 1806 he prophesied that in fifty years 'the American-English will be spoken by more people than all the other dialects of the language'. Mr. Mencken ran up his flag, 'The American Language', in 1919.

'Lovers and encouragers of American literature' were to be found in Boston in 1774. In 1865 the *Atlantic Monthly* judged it superfluous to refer 'to the rapid advance of

To What Strange Shores?

American literature'. In 1886 Howells feared 'we shall probably never have a great American novel as fancied by the fondness of critics'. Pure literature is, in fact, the weakest element in the quotations, from no fault in their selection, but because the best American writers—up to 1900—wrote in the classical tradition and tended to avoid Americanisms. *Americanism*—itself an Americanism, coined by Witherspoon in 1781, and not found in England before 1826—reflects this tendency, reminding us of the history of *Scotticism* in the eighteenth century. But in another sense *Americanism* was a national boast. Jefferson wrote of 'the dictates of reason and pure Americanism'. The word is not often used today in that sense, and *pure* has given way to *one hundred per cent*.

The price of such a work is important. It is expected to comprise about twenty parts, or approximately 2,400 pages, and the price is fixed at 17*s*. a part, which, if the estimate is correct, will be £17. But subscribers before 31 December 1936 may undertake to pay 12*s*. 6*d*. a part—say £12. 10*s*.—or may pay ten guineas down, with a corresponding addition or rebate if the work exceeds or falls short of the estimate. It is greatly to be hoped that many libraries in this country and the Dominions will elect to cash in—it should rather be cash out?—for immediate possession. The book is published on this side of the Atlantic by Sir Humphrey Milford, and may in some degree be claimed as an Oxford dictionary. It remains to commend the work of the Chicago University printers, who have produced a clear and legible page, from which the more important words are readily picked out. This is important, since the work

To What Strange Shores?

repays selective (if not continuous) reading, as well as mere reference.

Both *D.A.E.* and Mr. Mencken quote the prophecy of Daniel which is printed at the head of this article. The editors of *D.A.E.* point no moral; but Mr. Mencken boldly claims that modern American is closer to Shakespeare than so-called standard English, showing all the characters that marked the common tongue in the days of Elizabeth. His *American Language*, first published in 1919, has deserved the great popularity in the United States which has induced him, by successive revisions, so to expand it that it is now, with 800 full pages, more than twice its original bulk. That it has had relatively little circulation in this country is unfortunate, the more so as it is a far better guide to translation out of the American than to the composition of British English. Mr. Mencken's American is so good that he will seldom lead the British inquirer astray. His knowledge of English is also extensive; a remarkable feat, if we are right in our conjecture that it has been acquired without prolonged residence.

But his account of British equivalents will often take the American student either too far or not far enough. In part this follows from the very method which has made him so popular. Mr. Horwill treats, perhaps, 2,000 words in his 350 pages, giving a careful description of each and supporting it by quotations. Mr. Mencken's index contains over 10,000; and he deals with them not by way of a dictionary, but in a series of entertaining essays, in which half a dozen words may be paraded and dismissed in a single sentence. It is not possible to be accurate on such a scale. A good example is the attempt to deal with the terminology of the Universities in a page and a half. Mr. Mencken perhaps supposes, and certainly his innocent readers will infer, that all our universities are modelled on Oxford and Cambridge, having constituent colleges and Vice-Chancellors who 'serve for three years'. So we are led to believe that a high steward is a 'minor dignitary', 'that undergraduates are seldom called students', that *commencement*, except at Cambridge or Dublin, is called *degree-day* or *speech-day*, and that the British equivalent of *college boys* is *university-men*. (A *university man* is commonly not an undergraduate but a man who has had a university education.)

We add examples at random. *Swim-suit* is not, we hope, yet the normal English equivalent of *bathing-suit*; a *letter-box* is not properly a *pillar-box* unless it is a column, at least a pilaster, *marriage-lines* is dialect, vulgar, or jocular, not the normal English for *marriage-certificate*; a (fruit) *pie* is not necessarily a *tart*; we have yet to meet a motorist who calls a shock-absorber an *anti-bounce clip*; *walk the hospitals* has not displaced *study medicine*, it is a technical colloquialism; English *public schools* are not 'maintained chiefly by endowments' (as many know to their cost); nor is *council-school* the equivalent of U.S. *public school*; a member of Parliament does not *stand* (U.S. *run*) for office; since the offices to which he aspires are not elective, there is no formal candidature and therefore no *standing*; it is true, in the sense intended, that a candidate for Parliament 'is not *nominated*, but *adopted*', but strictly he is both; *cabinet* is not a synonym of *ministry*; solicitors *may* address parliamentary committees; Oxford men *go down* from Oxford, but not by the *down-train*; it is

To What Strange Shores?

true that '*car* never means a railway carriage', but the unit which we refrain from calling a *car* (unless it is a dining one) is not the *carriage* but the *coach*; it is true that 'flat-houses' are 'often *mansions*' in the sense that they are 'Belvedere Mansions', but not in the sense that any flat-dweller 'lives in a mansion'; it is unlikely that 'the sport of boating has given colloquial English the familiar term' *weir*; it is not true that we 'seldom speak of a *warm* day'.

Mr. Mencken acknowledges the 'Herculean struggles', on this part of his subject, of Mr. H. W. Seaman, of Norwich, England. But Mr. Seaman is perhaps not typical. He is the author of 'The Awful English of England', published in Mr. Mencken's own *American Mercury*, and is quoted (twice, pp. 328 and 609) as 'sick and tired of this so-called English accent', in which he finds 'a pansy cast' and 'a mauve, Episcopalian ring'. The advice of a more sympathetic English observer may, we hope, introduce some changes in Mr. Mencken's next edition.

Anything he especially contemns Mr. Mencken, like many others, is tempted to assign to Oxford. He is scornful of Oxford slang, 'a series of childish perversions'. It is true that our universities were never very fertile of slang; we think of 'school-boy slang' rather than of university slang; and the undergraduate if taxed with his poverty of invention might perhaps plead John Thorpe's excuse for the neglect of novel-reading, that he has something better to do. But Mr. Mencken will be glad to know that *brekker* is obsolete. *Jaggers*, we are assured, never meant St. John's. *A bit of a lad*, if it is of Oxonian origin, which seems very unlikely, is hardly the equivalent of 'the magnificent Ameri-

To What Strange Shores?

can *lounge-lizard*'. On the vexed question of 'standard English' and the 'Oxford accent', it was perhaps only to be expected that Mr. Mencken should accept the absurdities which have been widely propagated. But we rub our eyes when we find standard English, 'the dialect of a small minority', contrasted with American, 'a dialect spoken almost uniformly by nearly 125,000,000 people'. This is democracy indeed. Is there, then, no difference between Harvard and the Bronx? Is it really impossible to tell an American gentleman by his speech? In another place Mr. Mencken deplores the lack of any 'grammar of the daily speech of nearly 100,000,000 Americans'—that is, of 'vulgar American'—in which he tells us that the verb *write* is thus conjugated: 'I write', 'I written', 'I have wrote'.

But we would not give the impression that such imperfections seriously affect the value of the book. In the main it is a study of American speech, and therefore of American civilization, without any distorting reference to the British variety. On his own ground Mr. Mencken is a master, and his book is a storehouse of information and amusement.

The Yale Walpole[1]

'THE enormous and exquisite structure stands before us in all its Palladian beauty, and we can wander through it at our ease.' So wrote Lytton Strachey as he contemplated the sixteen volumes of Mrs. Paget Toynbee's edition of

[1] Review of the Yale Edition of Horace Walpole's Correspondence edited by Wilmarth Sheldon Lewis. Volumes 1 and 2, *Walpole's Correspondence with William Cole*, edited by W. S. Lewis and A. Dayle Wallace. Published (incomplete) in *T.L.S.* 30 Oct. 1937.

The Yale Walpole

Walpole's letters, published more than thirty years ago and expanded after her death, by her husband's piety, in three supplementary volumes. That edition was a notable advance on Peter Cunningham's, though it did not completely supersede it. The world now learns that the Yale University Press has set its hand to a far larger enterprise—a new edition which by including the letters written to Walpole will come near to doubling the bulk of the text, and by elaboration of commentary and indexes is expected to fill thirty or forty substantial octavos and to be some fifteen years in the making. This is the most ambitious project yet undertaken by the Yale school of English scholars of which Professor Tinker is the founder—and we do not forget the Boswellian researches to which Professor Pottle has devoted his life. If its event is equal to its promise, it may well eclipse the Variorum Shakespeare as the greatest achievement of editorial scholarship in the United States.

The enterprise has not been lightly undertaken. It now faces anticipatory criticism under the aegis of a great University Press, and fortified by the countenance of an Advisory Committee of fourteen experts. The committee includes eight English scholars and six Americans (we keep our lead, but the margin is narrow), with Professor Feuillerat in charge of Walpole's Gallic affinities. It is headed by Earl Waldegrave (still better known as Lord Chewton), whose adherence may be taken as implying dynastic approval—for Chewton Priory is in the direct line from Strawberry Hill; and it includes, besides experts in English literary scholarship, two historians in the technical sense, three librarians, and the Director of the National Portrait

The Yale Walpole

Gallery: eloquent testimony to the range of Walpole's accomplishment in politics, letters, antiquities, biography, typography, iconography.

But such work as this is not done by committees, however valuable their encouragement or reassuring their certificate. Such work can only be accomplished, as it can only be justified, by the impact of individual enthusiasm upon a chosen object. It has long been known to the curious in this country that Mr. Wilmarth Lewis was devoting exceptional talents and opportunities to the acquisition of the relics of Strawberry Hill, that vast accumulation of books, manuscripts, and 'curiosities' that was so widely, so lamentably dispersed by the provisions of Walpole's will and by the sale in 1842 of 'the classic contents' of his house. Mr. Lewis began where most collectors begin and end, with 'collectors' pieces', with the crockets and finials of Strawberry Gothic. The products of Walpole's private press have been collectors' game ever since it began work in 1757. Of these there were many copies with special attractions—Walpole's own annotated copies, or extra-illustrated copies which belonged to his friends. There were books from his collection, with the shelf-marks which reveal, on analysis, their very place in his library; most of these have his marginal jottings. There were endless prints, plans, and designs. There were occasional manuscripts. These things are of great interest and value, and without them the Yale edition would not have been what it will be. But they are rather decorative than structural. Only by degrees, as experience defined his vision, did Mr. Lewis work down to the foundations of Walpole's fame, to that portrait of an

The Yale Walpole

age which is embodied in a miscellaneous and seemingly casual correspondence. The development of his ambition is mirrored, for the curious gaze, in the *anecdota* which he has printed from his collection, in imitation and continuation of Walpole's own *Miscellaneous Antiquities*, a series of fragile scraps, and in the massive proportions, the sober magnificence, of the prospectus and the initial volumes of the Yale Edition of Walpole's Correspondence.

America has many collectors and many accomplished scholars. It is seldom that opportunity combines the roles. Mr. Lewis's adventure has therefore an unusual interest, since it exemplifies at once the American absorption of our heritage and the American challenge to our scholarship. It is true that in this photographic age, when many itinerant editors are equipped to 'shoot' their manuscripts at sight, editing is not, as it once was, geographically conditioned. But the influence of the great collections, and the uncommunicable magnetism of authentic originals, are still paramount. We must now recognize that the natural home of Walpolian studies is henceforth not at Cambridge or Twickenham, or even Bloomsbury, but in Connecticut.

The drift to America of rare or unique objects is a story of epic range, and the inquiry must here be limited to manuscripts and printed books. It has in this country been variously received and explained. Why, it is asked, do the Americans 'get everything'? Is it because they have more money, or because their desire to get is greater than ours to keep? Certainly they have more money, and still more money that they are free to spend. Certainly their historic sense gives them an imperious desire to take back with

The Yale Walpole

them some of those pieces of antiquity in which this country is still steeped, and of which America, with all its museums, is still pitifully bare. The invaders, moreover, do not merely exercise a privilege; they are, in their own eyes, fulfilling a responsibility. 'Everyone in a certain position owes it to the community to collect something', wrote the late George Apley in Mr. Marquand's recent satire. It is as unreasonable as it is ungenerous in us to sell, and then complain that they buy. If we talk of a national heritage, it is theirs as well as ours; and we ought not, as a nation, to grudge them a share; though there are some things which it is our right and our duty to keep at all costs.

But the change that is taking place in our time is not only a geographical redistribution of wealth; it is also a phase in the socialization of all records. Until the last century such records as survived were mainly in private hands. They were kept by that class of society which alone had the means of keeping them—the established families which, from generation to generation, occupied the same capacious houses. These had their libraries and muniment rooms, sometimes their librarians. Their successive owners developed a pride of possession, and the rudiments of a sense of duty. Even when conscious collecting became a common recreation, most of the collectors were of this class, and their private hoards were merged with the family heirlooms. So even Garrick's quartos found their way to Chatsworth. It was a rare accident that brought Malone's collection to Bodley, or Capell's to Trinity. Royal collections proved impermanent, and even the British Museum was of slow growth.

The Yale Walpole

The days of the noble collector are almost over. Economic changes have in our own time enormously depleted the great private collections on which the Historical Manuscripts Commission did its work. But the Englishman is still reluctant to alienate inherited treasures except under pressure; and when a man is pressed for money he wants the best price he can get. It is unreasonable to expect him to take less than the market price in the interests of a public library. The efforts of our libraries, which are slenderly endowed, and of the private societies called their Friends, can do no more than save a few scraps from the general ruin. If we are to go on complaining of our losses, it is time we exerted ourselves on a national scale to reduce them. The National Art Collections Fund has shown, in a neighbouring field, how much can be done to stem the tide. A few private collectors like the late Lord Brotherton have notably swelled our savings. But in this country such men are rare. The need for private or concerted action has long been seen. Even in the nineteenth century the compilers of Auction catalogues expressed pious hopes that this or that document 'might not leave the country', or 'might find a home in the National Collection'. Not very much has been done.

The American situation is radically different. Americans in general do not found new dynasties, and primogeniture is limited by public sentiment. The prejudice is strong against the private transmission of great collections, and this affects the whole attitude to private acquisition; for it is almost assumed that a collector is a custodian for his lifetime only, and that all tracks lead to the libraries. Again,

The Yale Walpole

the indirect contribution of the private collectors is seconded by the direct contribution of individuals to the libraries, in money or in kind, or to the funds spent on behalf of the libraries.

Two examples of such munificence are germane to our present subject. It is understood that the Lewis collection of Walpoliana will remain in the library built for it at Farmington, but will one day become an endowed department of the Yale University Library. The Associates of that Library, among whom Mr. Lewis is prominent, have in the last dozen years spent on rarities and luxuries, such as no library could well buy from its regular resources, a sum which reduces all our efforts in this kind to insignificance.

It is a relief to turn to the personal side of these international episodes. There are few British labourers in literary scholarship who are not indebted to the generous communication of American collectors and American dealers. The position of the British owner, and possible vendor, is more delicate, and his appropriate emotions are less simply definable. Yet we have the picture, drawn from life or from the pages of Henry James, of the American collector (and it would be affectation to ignore his charming wife or daughter), whose union of tact with simplicity, of kindliness with shrewdness, robs invasion of half its terrors. We harden our hearts to connive at looting, and find ourselves sharing a pious pilgrimage.

Mr. Lewis's preface and his notes (with their frequent 'now w.s.l.' printed in very small capitals) are eloquent of both co-operations. The work is strictly American in its execution, but it is largely British in its sources and in the minor contributions of special knowledge. Mr. Lewis's acknowledgements suggest that the grimmest portals have opened to his knock. They make it clear that British scholars have been eager to help him. On this plane at least the two civilizations are at one.

Even when the labours of discovery and acquisition were over (and will there ever be an end?) the editor and his advisers had to face many difficult problems. The mere mass of the text gives importance to technical questions of method which on a smaller scale are matters almost of indifference. The stoutest heart may quail when it is known that the tale of Walpole's correspondence has reached seven thousand; and it must be conceded that so vast and various a collection will find few to read it through. But the bulk of our material is not within our control, for here there can be no question of selecting. It is the more important that the enormous and exquisite structure should be furnished with adequate directions, that the visitor may find what he seeks and go away satisfied, not bewildered. Walpole compiled and printed an elaborate guide to Strawberry Hill, that his visitors might know what they were seeing. The Yale editors have the more formidable task of guiding us through his mind.

The wisdom of including both sides of a correspondence will not be doubted. The principle was applied to Walpole by Toynbee in his edition of the mutual correspondence of Gray, Walpole, West, and Ashton, from the Waller collection, and later in the supplementary volumes mentioned above. But Toynbee no more than scratched the surface. The Prospectus reveals over 1,500 letters, wholly or in part unpublished, from Mann, Montagu, Cole, Mason, and the Hertfords alone. It is fortunate, indeed, that so much has been preserved, for a letter and its answer are complementary, and the complete text may save a far greater bulk of dull or doubtful exegesis. Even if the other side is not very good in itself, it may be useful as a foil; for if Walpole's letters have a fault it is that they are too good, too consistently brilliant.

The decision to give all the letters is no doubt partly responsible for a second decision, which will be received with more hesitation—the decision to abandon chronology and to revert to the practice of the first editors, who printed the letters in separate correspondences. The chronological arrangement is to be preferred in dealing with the letters of a single writer; we follow his body and his mind from place to place and from thought to thought in temporal succession. But if the series is interrupted by letters from a score of correspondents, so that a letter may be separated from its answer by many other letters, with or without their answers—that indeed is like life, but it is not like art. The pattern may be intolerably intricate. An actual example given in the preface may be expressed symbolically thus: A to B, A to C, C to A, D to A, A to B, A to E, A to C, A to F, A to B, B to A, A to G.

In practice the editor had no choice; for this is a co-operative undertaking, and procedure by chronology would have meant either that each of a dozen workers must be equally conversant with every facet of Walpole's activities, or that the editor must face an impossible task of fitting detached pieces of work into sequence. The method chosen has obviated this, enabling each sub-editor to concentrate on a manageable section of the material. Convenience, moreover, required publication by instalments; for so vast a work could never be finished if it had to remain in manuscript for fifteen years. The editor has thus been able to plan his work with due regard to the state of his knowledge; for some correspondences are now plain sailing; he has everything, or is pretty sure that nothing remains in hiding; others are still beset with obscurity, clues leading to no certain issue. Inevitably the work will be complicated and embarrassed by discoveries which will come too late to fall in their proper place; but the method chosen will make that drawback as little as it can be made. There must in any case be a residuum of miscellaneous letters, and the order there will no doubt be that of date.

All this may seem to suggest that the arrangement adopted is, however necessary, a necessary evil. We believe that it will be found a positive good. Scepticism will hardly survive the appearance of the Cole correspondence. For Walpole's letters to Cole, printed without Cole's letters which alone make them intelligible, and scattered among thousands of others, can never have been read as a whole, or with much pleasure or profit, except by a few hardened medievalists. Now, completed in two volumes, they take on order and meaning, and become eminently readable. Cole's are fuller, and in many ways better, than Walpole's, for Cole was a real master of his subject. The correspondence has little more than two topics, the Middle Ages and the gout; and the same things recur: the same books, pedigrees, and epitaphs, the same symptoms and the same remedies.

The Yale Walpole

The editors' task has not been easy, but it has been straightforward, and their enjoyment of it is infectious. It has been their opportunity to put Cole in his true place among the garrulous antiquaries. The Bletchley diaries had taught us that he had that quality of concentration which may make a man of very ordinary parts a good diarist. The same quality made him an admirable correspondent; and the contrast between the two friends, the obscure plodder and the universal amateur, gives light and shade to their intercourse.

Once at least Cole's introspective absorption blossoms in a masterpiece of narrative. In his return from Cambridge, one December night in 1779, he was 'near demolished' by an indiscretion of his servant (ii. 180).

The case was this: the Master of Emmanuel, my very good friend, just recovered himself from death's door, as said commonly, invited me to dine with him on Monday. As I was very well, I went with pleasure to see him, meaning to come away when the moon was risen, but he much pressing me to stay and play a game at whist, and eat a piece of brawn only for supper, I was tempted to do so, though utterly against my practice, never tasting anything after tea for these twenty years, and staying supper at Cambridge but once, and that at Dr Lort's chambers seven years ago, for these twelve years. I stayed till eleven, and Mr Masters, my neighbour, being there also, we got into our separate carriages at the College Gate. It seems his driver was drunk, for about a mile on this side my house, I observed my driver turn about twice or three times to look behind him, and then jump down and run to the assistance of Mr Masters, who was making an horrible outcry, as his servant was under his horses' feet, and the horses trampling upon him. The instant my horses found themselves at liberty, with the reins on their backs, they set out a full gallop, and so continued till they passed through the turnpike in my village, which the gate-keeper had unluckily set wide open, not to interrupt me, on hearing the rattle of the wheels on the frost, though it then began to thaw, and was dripping rain. All this while I was seated at the bottom of the chaise, with my legs out of it, and resting on the footboard, with an intention to have jumped out, as occasion might offer, but observing the swiftness of the hinder wheels, was afraid of my gown's being entangled in it, and so might be dragged along after the carriage. I had let down all the glasses at first, and in doing so, somehow or other, had dropped my hat. This added to my fright, for always keeping myself so immoderately warm and hardly ever stirring out, I concluded if I escaped being dashed to pieces, I should certainly catch a bad cold and fever, being exposed so late to the wind and weather and without any hat. Providence, however, was more propitious to me than are my deserts, for the horses, being used to a good smooth road, galloped on without any ill accident the whole mile and cleared the turnpike, where the keeper standing and seeing no driver, he ran at full stretch and stopped the horses and saved my life, for had they gone a furlong further, to the short turn out of the road, to the lane leading to my house, where were two small road bridges and ugly ditches on each side, all had been over. Thank God, I got to bed in five minutes, and my servant, frightened to death, soon after came in also.

The main theme of the Cole correspondence is English antiquities, and the reviewer has to confess his incompetence to appraise a commentary on such a text. But there are ample indications that Dr. Wallace's work has been surely based, that he has known where to seek his information and how to present it. Mr. Lewis assumes responsi-

The Yale Walpole

bility for the notes, which he has revised and reduced to a common form of his own devising. It is clear that infinite pains, and much ingenuity, have been given to the design of these volumes, which of necessity lay down a pattern for all that are to follow.

The method of publication will certainly facilitate continuous reading. Few perhaps will read the Cole volumes through, except hardened antiquaries and the admirers of William Cole. Cole will be followed by Madame du Deffand, whom few but specialists in French social history will care to follow through 'five or six volumes'. It is believed that most of Walpole's letters to her have perished, and so the poor blind lady's monotony is almost unrelieved. But she is to be succeeded by George Montagu (263 letters to him, 161, unpublished, from him); there, all lovers of the social scene will be attracted.

Mr. Lewis tells us that Walpole, in a peculiar degree, kept his correspondents apart, and that this belonged to his plan; for he had a plan, and a plan for posterity. So on literature he wrote to Gray, and when he lost Gray, to Mason; on antiquities to Cole and later to Lort; on politics to Mann; on trifles to George Montagu, and later to Lady Ossory. It is due to a great artist that we should preserve his design from confusion.

But, the historian may ask, will the work be crowned not only by the general index promised by the prospectus, comprehending (and doubtless surpassing) the special indexes appended to each correspondence, but also by a chronological survey? One imagines a list ('24 July 1776, Walpole at Strawberry Hill to Cole at Milton'?) which would make

The Yale Walpole

it easy for (say) the political historian to exhaust the correspondence for Walpole's comments on the public events of a year. There might be fifty such entries to a page, and at that rate 7,000 letters could be covered in 140 pages. But much more information would be welcome; why not a volume? The scale on which the edition is planned is an invitation to call for more and more clues to the maze.

The first duty of an editor is to furnish a faithful text. The improvements on existing texts will not be the greatest service rendered by the Yale editors, who will supersede their predecessors mainly by their additions to the correspondence and by their commentary and other apparatus. But even here they will make a notable advance. Cunningham and the Toynbees relied largely on earlier printed texts, which had the usual faults of inaccurate transcription and editorial manipulation. Miss Berry in particular (in the 1798 collection of Lord Orford's Works) tampered with her originals in the interest of elegance and delicacy. Even Mrs. Toynbee, who may be classed as Victorian, was bound to suppress on occasion. The Yale editors are freed from all such restrictions. They are also incomparably better equipped by the possession of originals and photographs, and by Mr. Lewis's knowledge of Walpole's hand and his command of the resources of many libraries and many minds. We may expect a good text.

And what of the commentary? If justification is still needed for a new edition, it can be said simply that Walpole's letters have not yet been adequately annotated. Mrs. Toynbee's small octavos were meant for armchair reading, and her brief notes are biographical. They gave some indication of the persons of the drama, the many hundreds of Lord Johns and Lady Marys who cross the stage. But the letters teem with recondite allusions, and are not fully intelligible without an elaborate commentary. So long ago as 1848 the *Quarterly* reviewer of the letters to Lady Ossory complained that the editor had taken his duties too lightly, and had failed to give 'the explanations of small events, slight allusions, obscure anecdotes', without a knowledge of which 'his best letters would be little more than a collection of riddles'.

Is it worth while? Mr. Lewis has no misgivings. In his judgement the letters are the best possible foundation on which to build an encyclopaedic survey of the age. 'Sooner or later the eighteenth century scholar, be his subject what it may, must consult Walpole's correspondence.' The letters cover more than half the century, and except for theology, economics, music, and the natural sciences they deal with all the main divisions of English life—with politics, literature, art, manners, and historical inquiry. If this position is accepted, the commentary can hardly be too full. But the greater the mass of information supplied, the heavier is the editor's responsibility for its orderly arrangement and for the provision of all practicable aids. Mr. Lewis thinks of his edition as 'primarily a work of reference', and we may take him at his word. The embarrassing wealth of the material justifies, indeed it enjoins, preoccupation with questions of method. It is natural to speculate how a work on this scale can best be equipped with references, whether internal (cross-references) or external (index-references). One point readily occurs. Since the arrangement of the work does not observe chronology, it was clearly useless to give the letters of any section a consecutive numeration. It was equally impracticable to number the 7,000 in advance, since the tale is not yet complete—new letters are still being found. It was impossible to refer, by volume and page, to volumes yet unborn. The result is that the references are of the form 'See H W to Mason 9 Aug. 1779'. This is slightly more cumbrous than the more familiar form of reference to a numbered document or to a page; but it is much more informative, since it tells us, at sight, something of the nature of the evidence adduced. It is indeed a question whether the apparatus of scholarship has not suffered from excessive mechanization. References must of course be given, if only that reviewers and other experts may have the means of checking them. But it should be remembered that a merely mechanical reference means no more, to almost all readers, than a certificate by the editor, whose word they must accept, that he has evidence for a statement. A direction to 'see Letter 500' or 'see page 500', is hardly more than conventional, for we know that the reader is unlikely to comply. But if a reference is in some degree significant, a judicious reader will often be enlightened; a name or a date will give him, at the least, some hint of the nature of the evidence offered. In the case cited, it is apparent that the witness is Walpole himself. Such a citation is manifestly more valuable than a page-reference, which may prove to be to a secondary authority, such as an editorial note.

The problem of index-references is of course different, for an index is primarily, at least, a finder. But it is not always remembered that a finder is useless unless it finds. The index of names to the (eighteenth-century) *Gentleman's Magazine* was compiled mechanically from the annual indexes, which gave no christian names or initials. The article *Smith* is accordingly a huge maze of figures, which are useless. You can find a Montmorency, but you cannot find a Smith. The absurdity is here patent; but few indexes are wholly free from such absurdities on a smaller scale. It may be true to say that any number of *bare* references, in excess of half a dozen, expects too much of human patience. An index-article of any length, therefore, must be articulated somehow, if it is to be generally useful. If the attempt is made, it is quickly apparent that an index can be something much more than a means of finding a particular needle in a bottle of hay. It may be made a guide to the work and a conspectus of its contents; in its longer articles it may even be continuously readable. Now if an indexer aims at this kind of service, his ingenuity will suggest all sorts of ways in which information can be concisely conveyed or suggested.

The history of scholarship has many examples of such indexing. Professor Pottle has recently reminded us of the debt we owe to the anonymous compiler of the index to Nichols's *Literary Anecdotes*, a substantial volume much of which is readable. Professor Pottle himself, and his collaborators at Yale, have lately given us an index to the eighteen volumes of Boswell's journals, which we commend to all indexers as a model. It is designed for independent use, and will in fact be used in many libraries which do not contain the eighteen volumes.

The Yale Walpole

The Cole correspondence was a relatively simple matter for the indexer, and gives hardly a foretaste of the immense task which will confront the editors when they tackle the general index. The index compiled by Mrs. Mosely is, however, a substantial instalment in eighty pages, and seems thoroughly workmanlike. The persons are not merely named, they are defined and dated. The drawbacks of alphabetical arrangement are sometimes apparent, as when, in the article *Strawberry Hill*, *Terrace* is followed by *the setting* and *three owls*. But this article is otherwise well arranged, and its generous typographical disposition makes it easy for the reader to find his way through nearly 200 references.

The volumes are nobly designed by Mr. Rollins, and printed at the Yale University Press with great accuracy and beauty. The illustrations give a glimpse of the interest and variety of the Farmington collection.

It remains to congratulate the editor and publishers on the first-fruits of their preparatory labours, long and arduously sustained, and to wish them all prosperity in a task which concerns our people not less nearly than it concerns theirs. Walpole was a great Englishman and a great liberal. His age was a great formative age of American, as of English, civilization. He has been called the prince of letter-writers; he is also the most faithful of chroniclers, the most patient and the most comprehensive of commentators.

The Prospectus informs us that it is hoped to complete the edition in some fifteen years and in between thirty and forty volumes, for which subscriptions are invited at the rate of thirty-five shillings a volume. It is of course apparent that the return from sales can be but a small fraction of the cost of acquiring the materials and of compiling and producing the work. The first volume contains a list of nearly two hundred subscribers, public and private. In the circumstances it was not to be expected that Great Britain would furnish any large proportion of the subscribers. We hope that many British names will figure in later lists. Meanwhile the greatness of the subject and the devotion of the promoters are fittingly recognized; for the first name in the list of subscribers is that of H.M. King George the Sixth.

Ὅτι's Business[1]

Semper ego auditor tantum? might have been the motto of this elegant apology for the life of exact scholarship, this searching analysis of the Battle of the Books, of the Ancient Difference[2] between genius and scholarship, literature and learning. But only if its author had been a different kind of man. It has been argued from the silence of the *Oxford Book of Latin Verse* that he does not regard Juvenal as a poet. These lectures show no trace of Juvenal's or of Swift's *indignatio*. Readers of the *Oxford Magazine* know that the reviewer who signs himself H. W. G. can dip his pen, if not in vitriol then in the milder acids and subacids. But here, summing up for his lucky Cambridge auditors, his far more numerous readers, perhaps above all for himself, the broodings of a lifetime, Mr. Garrod has distilled no gall; everywhere is sweet reasonableness and natural Christianity.

[1] Review of H. W. Garrod, *Scholarship, its Meaning and Value.* Published (incomplete) as *The Scholar's Defence* in *T.L.S.* 25 Jan. 1947.
[2] Plato's παλαιὰ διαφορά.

"Ὅτι's Business

No man of our time is better equipped than Mr. Garrod of Merton to trace the long history of scholarship, to describe the activities and appraise the qualities of the scholar's life. An accomplished classic, he began his career by editing Latin poets, of whom he has compiled a standard anthology. In recent years he has exhibited to a small but cosmopolitan body of judges the width and depth of his Erasmian learning. But it is long since his attention was mainly directed to modern literature. His work has ranged from Donne to Wordsworth, and culminated in an elaborate edition of Keats. Yet he is still dissatisfied with his armoury, and in this book deplores his ignorance of Hebrew.

It was a sure instinct that led Mr. Garrod to start from the scholar who stands in the forefront of *The Vanity of Human Wishes*: that victim of 'Toil, Envy, Want, the Patron, and the Jail'. For his inaugural thesis is that at a date—he puts it, rather tentatively, soon after 1600—the modern divorce between Literature and Learning, between Genius and Scholarship, was complete. In Johnson therefore, who is later by a century, and who is in many ways typical of the age he dominates, we should find a test-case. In another sense, moreover, Johnson is not typical but exceptional, since he was at once genius and scholar, lexicographer and poet. His case should therefore furnish double corroboration of the thesis; if the two partners can be separated in him, the decree of divorce is absolute indeed. It may be argued that, on the main issue, while Housman's case would support Mr. Garrod, Johnson's tends to confute him; is it really possible to draw a rigid frontier between the poet and the lexicographer, or between the 'little lives' (so he called them) and 'little prefaces' that merge biographical research and aesthetic judgement in the *Lives of the Poets*? The objection assumes, of course, that aesthetic criticism lies in the literary not in the scholarly province. On the minor issue of chronology it may be argued that Mr. Garrod's date is a good deal too early. In the common parlance of the eighteenth century (which Mr. Garrod knows less well than he knows the seventeenth or the nineteenth?) Literature and Learning are complements not opposites. As late as Charles Lamb's time a (doubtless old-fashioned) critic, when the question was of the two greatest names in English literature, could presume that the answer must be, not Shakespeare and Milton, not even Dryden and Pope, but 'Sir Isaac Newton and Mr. Locke'.

Mr. Garrod lays stress on Johnson's failure, in his portrait of the scholar, to include one essential ingredient, unselfishness. 'Of learning as an end in itself, of a scholarship which is its own reward, Johnson has nothing to say.' That is true of the scholar in the *Vanity*. It is perhaps not true of Johnson, who jestingly called himself 'a pedant'; who 'liked that muddling work' of making dictionaries; who always let the booksellers cheat him; who insisted that there is no such thing as useless knowledge. The explanation of the discrepancy is perhaps this, that in his poem Johnson's attention is focused on the vanity of ambition: of worldly or other-worldly aspirations. The poem itself declares, in its concluding portrait of the good man, that not all aspirations are doomed to frustration. The point is important, if only because Johnson is a scholar *manqué*, or if you like it better, a scholar rescued for higher ends.

″Οτι's Business

Given some differences of opportunity and some of temperament, he might have been one of the world's greatest scholars, a rival to Bentley. Even as it is, the scholarship of the Dictionary amounts to genius, and Johnson has been called Shakespeare's best editor. His considered opinion of scholarship is phrased in terms of veneration: 'Conjectural criticism has been of great use in the learned world; nor is it my intention to depreciate a study that has exercised so many mighty minds, from the revival of learning to our own age.' Emendatory criticism, he somewhere writes, demands more than human powers.

Mr. Garrod advances, and proves from his own experience, what will be thought a paradox: that 'consummate learning is a good deal more rare than genius'. He has, in half a century spent in academic cloisters, 'known genius familiarly'. Perhaps F. H. Bradley was uppermost in his mind when he wrote this; but other names readily occur—is not Mr. Eliot a Merton man? On the other hand, 'consummate learning I have met only very rarely, conversing with it uncomfortably, and often not well knowing what it would be at'. Was Ingram Bywater in his mind? Another example of his last point comes pat. Henry Bradley was a man of consummate learning (and a Hebraist). Robert Bridges was a man of genius. They loved each other dearly, and may be said to have collaborated; yet it has been justly said that R.B. never began to understand what H.B.'s work was about.

This relative frequency is one reason why the world, which holds out both hands to genius, is unhappy in the presence of scholarship: suspicious, often contemptuous, sometimes even resentful. 'There is nothing in the method of it by which it can capture the heart.' The whole passage is knit close with wisdom. The writer of this article is moved to illustrate an august theme from the morsel of his private experience. He is sometimes reproached, by his family and friends, for devoting to the niceties of scholarship talents that, they kindly hint, are worthy of a loftier flight. His reply is that, if he has not 'known genius familiarly', he has known dozens of people who could write, say, readable essays, and some who could write very good ones. He has known few whom he could trust to make the best use of the delicate tools of editorial scholarship.

We come now to the crux. What *is* the Ancient Difference? What are the windows of the soul from which Genius and Learning look on the world? Mr. Garrod (deprecating any charge of grandiloquence) finds that Genius and Learning share the knowledge of 'a broken unity of the human spirit'. But 'to genius this broken unity appears mainly as a moral and personal disaster. To learning it presents itself as an intellectual trouble.' Genius, finding the time out of joint, would mend it by intuition, by divination. Learning, equally conscious of the discontinuity of tradition, of the 'accidents of time, language, place and race' that 'hinder sympathy and understanding', seeks a different remedy. Endlessly patient and laborious, it tries to heal the breach by piecing together minute particles of evidence. Only to traditionalists, perhaps, will Mr. Garrod's diagnosis seem wholly adequate. But it does account for the quarrel, and explains why the world always takes the same side; it 'sides

*Ὅτι's Business

naturally with . . . the spiritual valour which dashes itself to pieces on the unbreachable walls which fence Truth', and has little sympathy with 'the slow and cautious movement of learning'. The history of our time has taught us to ask if the world might not get on better if it ceased to produce great men of action. It is at least a fair question whether speculative genius be not also a mixed boon.

From these heights Mr. Garrod descends to the lower levels of his subject, the history of scholarship. He is at pains to give the term accurate definition. To classical antiquity he allows, at the most, the merest rudiments. Every writer except the first is a scholar in the sense that he is aware of not being the first, in some degree conscious of a tradition. But Mr. Garrod will not call Plato a scholar, nor even Aristotle. Aristotle is not conscious that he is one kind of being, classifying and criticizing poets who belong to another order of being. The organization and codification of learning was given to the world by the Alexandrians. Aristarchus was a scholar in the sense that he recognized Homer as something his editor could not aspire to be. But Mr. Garrod is not satisfied yet; he does not find in Alexandria that fixed gulf between original and commentary which is his differentia of scholarship. This was unknown to the middle ages; Mr. Garrod might have quoted Caxton: 'that noble poete and grete clerke Vyrgyle.' He would date it from the Renaissance, though without insisting on any precise chronology. His reviewer is not competent to do more than hint a suspicion that he is less than just to the Middle Ages when he accepts the word renaissance at its strictest significance. Is it really true that 'the energies of Western Europe' had been 'long dormant'? Is it 'bare truth to say that the movement out of which sprang what we call scholarship sought, not learning, but life'?

However that may be, when the great Italians get to work on the precious manuscripts of a vanished age, scholarship is on the march. Mr. Garrod traces its long, laborious journey, full of the tedium of drudgery, the pangs of disappointed ambition, the rancours of rivalry; but full also of the thrills of discovery and the triumphs of achievement. In detailing the itinerary of scholarship Mr. Garrod is in a way retracing his own footsteps. He lingers affectionately on the work of the pioneers, Petrarch and Poggio, Aldus and Valla, the men who first collated manuscripts and tried to write like Cicero. He discusses, of course, *ipse Erasmianissimus*, how Erasmus by his edition of the New Testament 'broke down for good and all the barriers between sacred and profane learning'. He raises reverent eyes to the inaccessible peaks of learning: to Scaliger, who by his incursion into the field of calendar reform became a force in European politics, and by the vast range of his knowledge linked East to West, and 'brought into the world the conception of the unity of history'; to Bentley (editor like himself of Horace and Manilius), who by his vernacular conduct of classical controversy split the literary world of England into factions, and provoked 'the Battle of the Books'. He glances at English latinity (*interprete Johanne Sparrow*) and deplores our failure to find our own language good enough when we pay homage to the fallen. He comes in the end to our own times, to the age of Bywater and Murray; and here are arresting digressions—if they are digressions—on

*Ὅτι's Business

translation, on the vices of Greek tragedy, on the evil consequences of our ignorance of Hebrew. This, interesting as it is, is the weakest part of a good book. It is Mr. Garrod's weakness that he loves a paradox. He may, being an honest man, discard a paradox he has entertained, seeing it to be false. It may be guessed that he does so with reluctance. Of the startling, shocking theses in this section some are very good, some are ponderable,—*sunt mala plura*? In the passages that debunk Attic literature in general (Plato 'is not Attic') and Attic tragedy and the metre of its dialogue in particular, Aeschylus and Thucydides are not named. Is this inadvertence or naughtiness?

There, to our disappointment, he stops short. We had hoped, as we turned the pages (all too few), that we should find illuminating parallels, ingenious discriminations, between the scholarship that deals with the dead languages and the scholarship that deals with our own: some account of the dealings of himself and others with Shakespeare, or Donne, or Johnson, or Keats. Perhaps in a later edition (there will surely be two, there ought to be more) we may learn from a fourth chapter whether, in Mr. Garrod's considered opinion, English scholarship (in the sense defined) has made good its claim to be so named.

The New Smith[1]

THIS impressive work of nearly 1,000 quarto pages is known by its preface to have a history dating from 1933, not without vicissitudes, from death or preoccupation, in its imposing group of editors, sub-editors, and super-editors. In the roll of its 161 contributors Oxford is naturally predominant, and the paucity of names from America may be noted with regret. The frequency, on the other hand, of Germanic names reflects the profits of our hospitality in these stricken years and recalls the great days of Gaisford, when the Oxford Press opened its doors to Continental learning.

The purpose of the compilation is not otherwise declared than by a modest comparison of it to the famous dictionary (1842) of Sir William Smith. This suggests that the promoters had in view a public consisting mainly of serious students, from the precocious schoolboy upwards, but embracing also those amateurs whose classical reach exceeds their grasp and those who would like to rub off accumulated rust. The scope of the work may be indicated by a sample. The fifty pages given to words beginning with D contain some 250 articles (which by rule of three gives 5,000 as a total). Of these twenty-one concern mythological persons, 151 real persons, fifteen places (thus avoiding the tendency of encyclopaedias to give too much space to geography). The remaining sixty-six articles deal with a rich variety of topics, religious, political, legal, literary, scientific, artistic, or domestic. Among these are dancing, de-

[1] *T.L.S.* 2 Apr. 1949: Review of the *Oxford Classical Dictionary*.

The New Smith

clamation, dedication, the Delian League, the Delphic oracle, democracy, dentistry, dialectic, dialect, dialogue, dicing, dictator, digesta, dithyramb, divination, dogs, Dorians, drama, dress, and dying. In their regard to the average reader's average attainment the editors and contributors seem to be judicious. The assumption properly varies with the subject-matter. Thus the article on Greek grammar is peppered with Greek words which are not explained; but no one is likely to be curious about Greek grammar who is ignorant of Greek. On the other hand, Mr. Denniston in his masterly sketch of Greek metre, though he assumes knowledge of the feet—dactyls, and so forth—does not assume knowledge of the various *cola*, such as the glyconic. Sometimes it may be thought that the need for drastic compression has led contributors to assume more knowledge than many readers command. In the article on the Latin language (from the bibliography of which the name of Lindsay is strangely absent) we are told of the disappearance of the consonant w and consonantal y, of the characteristic formation of the superlative in -smmos, and of the disappearance of nonthematic conjugations; this information will leave some accomplished Latinists guessing.

The treatment is severely factual. Even in writing of Sappho, pre-eminently a subject inviting flowers, Dr. Bowra almost confines his article to an enumeration of the subjects and metres of her (all but lost) seven 'books', permitting himself a single sentence in which to claim for her 'unequalled directness and power'. His article on Homer is devoted to the Homeric 'question', and gives only inci-

The New Smith

dental comments on what Kingslake calls 'the strong vertical light of Homer's poetry' or on 'the surge and thunder of the *Odyssey*'. But preoccupation with trees is in general not allowed wholly to hide the wood. Dr. Pickard-Cambridge in his treatment of Aeschylus is copious on the poet's theology, his plots and characters, his style, his 'pictures of incomparable beauty'. (It is misleading to describe the work of Walter Headlam as 'translation'. Headlam's crib was a peg on which he hung a substantial and important commentary.) Mr. Robinson spends little space on stylometric and other criteria for the order of Plato's dialogues; his article is mainly an attractive account of Plato's 'divine philosophy' and artistic genius. In 'Britannia' (an article to which many will turn) Mr. Stevens concentrates his limited space on an analysis of the degree to which the invaders were able to romanize this island. He does not quite tell us why we do not speak Latin. An example of a too esoteric article is that on vase-painting, a wilderness of names and technical terms, from which the reader does not learn the shapes of the vases, or what they were used for, or how they were painted. The article on Greek coinage will interest historians and economists; no one reading it would guess that the best Greek coins are among the most beautiful small objects that man has fashioned. An outstanding feat of compression is achieved by Dr. Tod on Greek epigraphy, where four columns of text are fortified by ninety-nine items of bibliography.

Exemplary specimens of the good judgement shown in the dictionary at its best are the articles on the Greek dialects and on Greek metre. Mr. Palmer makes it clear that

The New Smith

what are commonly called dialects are not the true local dialects of the inscriptions, but conventional literary forms, which so appropriated a given literary kind that all writers of that kind, wherever they lived, wrote in that dialect. It was because the Dorians invented the choric ode that the Attic tragedians were bound to 'give their language a Doric flavour' in that part of a play; in fact there is nothing Doric in the tragic choruses except the substitution of long *alpha* for *eta*. Ionic, again, invented and therefore monopolized history and science, and that is why Thucydides avoided such Attic provincialisms as the double *tau*. Mr. Denniston's sketch of Greek metre is necessarily packed with detail; but he is full and clear, shirking no difficulty, on the broad questions of principle that arise. Thus he states the case for and against the existence in Greek verse of that metrical stress or 'ictus' which we invariably, perhaps inevitably, give it, and concludes that the question is not settled. Yet he reassures us against the nihilism which insists that as we cannot know how Greek verse was said or sung, therefore we cannot appreciate its melodies; he is not afraid to tell us that Aeschylus in a certain passage 'turns the fourth paeon to magnificent account', or that 'the swing from iambics to trochaics is capable of charming effects'.

The favourers of classical studies may take some heart from this book. The classics are, in this country, relatively less important than they were, and their continuance is threatened. The *Oxford Classical Dictionary* will not become, like Smith, a household word. But classical learning and education have never, in their long history, been in the hands of scholars better equipped with learning, judgement, and good taste.

PR
442
C5
1971

Date Due

DEC 17			

LIBRARY
UNIVERSITY OF PUGET SOUND
Tacoma, Washington

PRINTED IN U.S.A.